EXERCISES IN PSYCHOLOGICAL TESTING

SECOND EDITION
EXERCISES IN PSYCHOLOGICAL TESTING

George C. Thornton III and Eugene R. Oetting

Colorado State University

HARPER & ROW, PUBLISHERS, New York

Cambridge, Philadelphia, San Francisco,
London, Mexico City, São Paulo, Sydney

1817

Sponsoring Editor: George A. Middendorf
Project Editor: Nora Helfgott
Cover and Text Designer: Robert Bull
Senior Production Manager: Kewal K. Sharma/Jacqui Brownstein
Compositor: Waldman Graphics Incorporated and Allyn-Mason, Incorporated
Printer and Binder: The Murray Printing Company
Art Studio: Vantage Art, Inc., Soho Studio, Inc.

Exercises in Psychological Testing, Second Edition

Library of Congress Cataloging in Publication Data

Thornton, George C., 1940–
    Exercises in psychological testing.

    1. Psychological tests—Problems, exercises, etc.
I. Oetting, E. R. (Eugene Richard), 1929–
II. Title.
BF176.T47   1981   150′.27′7   81-6839
ISBN 0-06-044909-8   AACR2

Contents

Preface

These exercises are designed to provide the student with experiences relevant to understanding the concepts involved in psychological testing. The student learns by engaging in the activities of the professional psychologist using tests. The student learns to administer group and individual tests, to score tests, to construct scales by item analysis, to develop norms, and to evaluate reliability and validity. In all of these activities, the student deals with materials and procedures similar to those involved in actual testing situations. Confidential test materials are not exposed, however; nor is the student presented with test norms that can be used to "analyze the personality" or "test the IQ" of friends.

We have made several changes in the second edition of this workbook. Revisions to previous exercises have eliminated redundancy and simplified the work for students and instructors. Increased emphasis has been placed on the development and analysis of achievement tests of knowledge. New exercises have been included dealing with differential validity, discrimination, performance tests, and behaviorally anchored rating scales for observation.

It is assumed that the student has had some introduction to elementary statistics, but statistical analyses have been kept in very simple forms. Statistics are used only where the meaning of the test data can best be brought out with statistical analyses.

The exercises are not designed to follow a textbook in a chapter-by-chapter fashion. Certain fundamentals of psychological testing are illustrated in an interesting and informative manner throughout the series of exercises. Discussion resulting from the exercises involves principles and procedures explained or illustrated in several textbooks. (See the table on page viii.) In a sense, the workbook makes textbook material alive and enjoyable. At the same time, the empirical scientific approach to the construction, validation, and interpretation of psychological tests is strongly emphasized.

As the student works with the test materials in this manual, he or she should be constantly alert for inadequacies they may contain. The directions for administering and scoring the tests may not deal with every problem that arises; there may be errors in the items measuring factual knowledge; more than one alternative may be correct for objective items; and the wording of items may be ambiguous. All of these are problems that must be faced by a person constructing or using a test; many of them are not solved adequately by published tests currently on the market. Discovering the "errors" in the tests in *Exercises in Psychological Testing,* Second Edition, and suggesting solutions for them, will be a valuable learning experience for the student.

Suggestions for maximizing the learning experiences from the use of *Exercises in Psychological Testing,* Second Edition, appear in the accompanying *Instructor's Manual* available to the instructor. Here the instructor will find discussions of the principles of measurement, practical suggestions for conducting the exercises, ways of contracting or expanding the exercises, and tips on how to change the potentially frustrating experience of encountering the "inadequacies" or "errors" in the tests into true learning experiences.

The authors wish to thank the following people who helped with the preparation of exercises in this revision: Rich Shikiar, Terry Dickinson, Gerry Glebocki, David Waldman, and Mike Ryan. Our special thanks go to Beth Telgenhoff who typed repeated changes in the exercises and so very carefully proofread the material.

GEORGE C. THORNTON III
EUGENE R. OETTING

Suggested Reading Assignments

	Anastasi	*chapter*	Brown	Cronbach	Gronlund	Mehrens and Lehmann	Thorndike and Hagan
Exercise 1	32–37	2	27–31, 56–62	44–114	249–263, 367–373	315–320	561–565
Exercise 2	67–102	4	174–201	82–113	387–424	133–156	113–149
Exercise 3	32–44	2	27–31, 56–62	44–114	249–263, 367–373	315–322	555–556, 560–565
Exercise 4	103–133	5	51–62, 67–96	151–179	105–125	87–103	73–94
Exercise 5	198–226	8	278–283		98–99, 110, 113, 120–121, 153–155, 265–267	191–193, 324–329	214–216
Exercise 6	134–140	6	122–128	145–148, 294–297	64–66, 81–84, 135–151, 164–209	110–112, 174–178, 274–290	198–245
Exercise 7	198–206, 211–213	8	278–281		153–160, 265–271	323–334	251–255
Exercise 8	140–151	6	97–121	126–142	82, 84–93	112–129	60–70
Exercise 9	90–197	4-8	109–110	406–451	553–556	674–681	617–618
Exercise 10	496–506, 529, 538–539	17,18	362–382	460–463		550–558	
Exercise 11	219–221	8	118	433–434			
Exercise 12	565–569, 576–585	19	393–401	651–654	470	580–581	498–501
Exercise 13	593–598	20	401–406	646–649, 675–678			501–506
Exercise 14	609–611	20		571–584	435–445	354–364	448–466
Exercise 15	96–100, 131–133	4,6	202–207, 246–248	84–85	18–20, 31–33, 142–143, 153–154, 271–274	49–61, 106–107, 129–130, 178–179, 201–202, 333–334	94–98, 166–176, 182–188
Exercise 16	417–422	14	287–290	248–251	494–499		166–177
Exercise A	68–71, 78–80	4	36–38, 180–183	89–94	398–401, 539–553	76–79, 143–144	33–40, 124–137
Exercise B	72–73, 80–88	4	39–42, 184–190	94–101	543–545, 551–553	79–81, 145–147	40–46, 129–137
Exercise C	104–110	5	42–45	128–135	85–88, 553–556	81–85	47–52

EXERCISES IN PSYCHOLOGICAL TESTING

LABORATORY EXERCISE 1

The Administration and Scoring of Individual General Ability Tests

PURPOSE

The purpose of this exercise is to give the student experience in giving and scoring individually administered tests. Discussion of and practice with test items will illustrate the importance of standardized procedures. The problems of establishing rapport, motivating the person being examined without providing cues of information, and finding the sources of inaccuracy in scoring will be encountered. Scores on a test are comparable only if standardized conditions are maintained for all examinees.

INDIVIDUAL GENERAL ABILITY TEST

The manual of the *Individual General Ability Test* contains a statement of its purpose and instructions for administration. As the student administers the Individual General Ability Test (IGAT), he or she should be concerned that each examinee is treated in the same manner. All individuals should be given the test in comfortable surroundings, free from distractions, and with ample workspace. The examiner should ensure that the person is not overly tired and is highly motivated to do well. In giving directions, the examiner should follow the test manual as closely as possible. When the instructions in the manual do not provide answers to special circumstances and questions which arise, the examiner will have to use judgment about the appropriate way to respond. Scoring the IGAT requires judgment on the part of the examiner for several items. The rules contained in the manual should be followed to ensure standard treatment of all persons being tested.

Notice: The Individual General Ability Test is not a true intelligence test, but parts of it are very much like sections of individual intelligence tests used by psychologists. Other parts of the IGAT are unusual; however, these parts are related to certain intellectual functions and are included to illustrate the variety of tests that can be used. Other parts are purposely constructed to illustrate *inappropriate* practices which are sometimes encountered in commercially available tests. In essence, the IGAT is designed to teach college students about individual intelligence testing without having to use test materials that are highly confidential. A score on this test is *not* an intelligence score. There is no existing evidence that scores on the IGAT are related to any significant variables or measures of ''success,'' such as academic performance, occupational effectiveness, or adjustment to life.

The problems on this test are designed to be given to college students. They are intended to be difficult, but interesting. The questions are probably not appropriate for noncollege people.

SUGGESTED READINGS

Anastasi, A. *Psychological Testing* (4th ed.). New York: Macmillan, 1976, pp. 32–37.

Brown, F. G. *Principles of Educational and Psychological Testing* (2nd ed.). New York: Holt, Rinehart and Winston, 1976, pp. 27–31, 56–62.

Cronbach, L. J. *Essentials of Psychological Testing* (3rd ed.). New York: Harper & Row, 1970, pp. 44–114.

Gronlund, N. E. *Measurement and Evaluation in Teaching* (3rd ed.). New York: Macmillan, 1976, pp. 249–263, 367–373.

Mehrens, W. A., and Lehmann, I. J. *Measurement and Evaluation in Education and Psychology* (2nd ed.). New York: Holt, Rinehart and Winston, 1975, pp. 315–320.

Thorndike, R. L., and Hagan, E. *Measurement and Evaluation in Psychology and Education* (4th ed.). New York: Wiley, 1977, pp. 561–565.

Recording Sheet
for Individual General Ability
Test: College Level

A. Analogies: Score

   Rooster ———————————————   ————
   Earth ——————————————————   ————
   Music ——————————————————   ————
   Pickup —————————————————   ————
      Total Analogies   ════

V. Vocabulary   Score

   dominant ————————————————
   ————————————————————————
   ————————————————————————   ————
   element ——————————————————
   ————————————————————————
   ————————————————————————   ————
   exotic ———————————————————
   ————————————————————————   ————
   arachnid ————————————————
   ————————————————————————
   ————————————————————————   ————
   ecdysiast ———————————————
   ————————————————————————
   ————————————————————————   ————

	Raw Score
Information	————
Analogies	————
Vocabulary	————
Letter Memory	————
Total Verbal	————

	Raw Score
Number Series	————
Spatial Relations	————
Object Relations	————
Sign Language	————

I. Information: Score

  1. ———————————————————   ————
  2. ———————————————————   ————
  3. ———————————————————   ————
  4. ———————————————————   ————
  5. ———————————————————   ————
  6. ———————————————————   ————
  7. ———————————————————   ————
  8. ———————————————————   ————
  9. ———————————————————   ————
  10. ——————————————————   ————
  11. ——————————————————   ————
  12. ——————————————————   ————
     Total Information   ════

M. Letter Memory: Check Series Repeated Correctly

     MQR   ————
     PLBT   ————
     KZMPD   ————
     BLKJTQ   ————
     ZKLDBRT   ————
     KDBLFRTP   ————
     RPTKDBJLF   ————
     CNTKPZFBLQ   ————

   Total Letter Memory ════

N. Number Series:

		Score
2, 4, 8, 16, ____, ____		_____
6, 9, 7, 10, ____, ____		_____
8, 6, 4, 2, ____, ____		_____
16, 8, 4, 14, ____, ____		_____

Total Number Series ══════════

O. Object Relations:

	Score
Size	_____
Distance	_____
Location	_____
Relative size	_____

Total Object Relations ══════════

S. Spatial Relations:

Paper	Score
4 × 4	_____
Third	_____
Clock	
Reversal	_____
Numbers	_____
Hands	_____

Total Spatial Relations ══════════

L. Sign Language

	+ or −	Score
Line 1	____	_____
2	____	_____
3	____	_____
4	____	_____
5	____	_____
6	____	_____
7	____	_____
Time Bonus		_____

Total Sign Language ══════════

Recording Sheet for Individual General Ability Test: College Level

A. Analogies: Score

    Rooster_____   _____
    Earth_____   _____
    Music_____   _____
    Pickup_____   _____

      Total Analogies   ========

	Raw Score
Information	_____
Analogies	_____
Vocabulary	_____
Letter Memory	_____
Total Verbal	_____

V. Vocabulary   Score

    dominant _____   _____

    _____   _____

    element _____

    _____   _____

    exotic _____

    _____   _____

    arachnid _____

    _____   _____

    ecdysiast _____

    _____

    _____

	Raw Score
Number Series	_____
Spatial Relations	_____
Object Relations	_____
Sign Language	_____

I. Information: Score

   1. _____   _____
   2. _____   _____
   3. _____   _____
   4. _____   _____
   5. _____   _____
   6. _____   _____
   7. _____   _____
   8. _____   _____
   9. _____   _____
  10. _____   _____
  11. _____   _____
  12. _____   _____

      Total Information   ========

M. Letter Memory:

	Check Series Repeated Correctly
MQR	_____
PLBT	_____
KZMPD	_____
BLKJTQ	_____
ZKLDBRT	_____
KDBLFRTP	_____
RPTKDBJLF	_____
CNTKPZFBLQ	_____
Total Letter Memory	========

19

N. Number Series:

                         Score

2, 4, 8, 16, ____ , ____   _____

6, 9, 7, 10, ____ , ____   _____

8, 6, 4, 2, ____ , ____   _____

16, 8, 4, 14, ____ , ____   _____

Total Number Series   _____

O. Object Relations:

                         Score

Size   _____

Distance   _____

Location   _____

Relative size   _____

Total Object Relations   _____

S. Spatial Relations:

Paper   Score

4 × 4   _____

Third   _____

Clock

Reversal   _____

Numbers   _____

Hands   _____

Total Spatial Relations   _____

L. Sign Language

                + or −   Score

Line 1   ____   _____

2   ____   _____

3   ____   _____

4   ____   _____

5   ____   _____

6   ____   _____

7   ____   _____

Time Bonus   _____

Total Sign Language   _____

Recording Sheet
for Individual General Ability
Test: College Level

A. Analogies: Score

    Rooster_____ _____
    Earth_____ _____
    Music_____ _____
    Pickup_____ _____

       Total Analogies   =========

	Raw Score
Information	_____
Analogies	_____
Vocabulary	_____
Letter Memory	_____
Total Verbal	_____

V. Vocabulary   Score

    dominant_____
    _____ _____

    element_____
    _____ _____

    exotic_____
    _____ _____

    arachnid_____
    _____ _____

    ecdysiast_____
    _____ _____

	Raw Score
Number Series	_____
Spatial Relations	_____
Object Relations	_____
Sign Language	_____

I. Information: Score

    1. _____ _____
    2. _____ _____
    3. _____ _____
    4. _____ _____
    5. _____ _____
    6. _____ _____
    7. _____ _____
    8. _____ _____
    9. _____ _____
    10. _____ _____
    11. _____ _____
    12. _____ _____

       Total Information   =========

M. Letter Memory: Check Series Repeated Correctly

	Check Series Repeated Correctly
MQR	_____
PLBT	_____
KZMPD	_____
BLKJTQ	_____
ZKLDBRT	_____
KDBLFRTP	_____
RPTKDBJLF	_____
CNTKPZFBLQ	_____
Total Letter Memory	=======

N. Number Series:

                  Score

2, 4, 8, 16, _____ , _____   _____

6, 9, 7, 10, _____ , _____   _____

8, 6, 4, 2, _____ , _____   _____

16, 8, 4, 14, _____ , _____   _____

.Total Number Series   ======

O. Object Relations:

                  Score

Size   _____

Distance   _____

Location   _____

Relative size   _____

Total Object Relations   ======

S. Spatial Relations:

Paper   Score

4 × 4   _____

Third   _____

Clock

Reversal   _____

Numbers   _____

Hands   _____

Total Spatial Relations   ======

L. Sign Language

             + or −   Score

Line 1   ____   _____

      2   ____   _____

      3   ____   _____

      4   ____   _____

      5   ____   _____

      6   ____   _____

      7   ____   _____

Time Bonus   _____

Total Sign Language   ======

Assignment for **EXERCISE 1**

1. Administer the IGAT to *five* college students.
2. Score the tests and record the scores in the appropriate spaces on the answer sheet.
3. Answer the following questions:
   a. List three factors which should be standardized in test administration.

   b. Why is it important to follow the directions given in a test manual and to use the scoring standards provided?

   c. Which items (if any) do you think might be biased or unfair to minorities or persons of low socioeconomic status? Why would they be unfair?

   d. How did you improve as you gave the test to subsequent examinees?

Construction of Norms and Test Profiles

PURPOSE

This exercise is designed to illustrate the computation of percentile scores and the preparation and interpretation of test profiles. Norms are compiled for each of the eight subtests of the Individual General Ability Test (IGAT). The test results for individuals are recorded on profile sheets to graphically represent performance on the various sections of the test. The student can then explain the test results to people examined earlier.

INTERPRETING SCORES

The raw score on a test or subtest has no meaning by itself. Several methods can be used to give meaning to the raw score, including:

1. *Norms*. An individual's raw score can be compared with scores of other people on the same test. *Norms* show the distribution of scores obtained by a standardization group. We can tell whether the individual performed above average, about in the middle, or below average when comparing the score with those of other people. This method is illustrated in the present exercise.
2. *Criterion validation*. An individual's score on the test is interpreted in terms of predicted performance on some other nontest behavior called a *criterion*. With this method, we must establish that scores on the test are related to performance on the criterion. For example, we might find that scores on a college entrance examination are related to grade-point average earned in subsequent university courses. Then we would be able to say that an individual who scored high on the test could be expected to succeed in the university with a certain probability. This method is illustrated in Exercise 8.
3. *Domain-referenced measurement*. An individual's performance on the test is compared with a predetermined set of standards for performance in a specifically defined domain. An example is a set of mathematical skills associated with addition, subtraction, multiplication, and division. With this method, individuals find out how their skills compare with some hierarchy of skills. Domain-referencing procedures are illustrated in Exercise 15.

NORM GROUP

The norm group for this exercise are those individuals who were tested by the entire class with the IGAT in Exercise 1. (Alternatively, the instructor may give the class a set of data gathered in another situation.) The scores for these individuals on each of the eight subtests will be compiled to provide the norms.

PERCENTILES AND PERCENTILE RANKS

The most common method of comparing test scores is the use of percentiles. *Percentiles* show the position of a given score in a distribution by stating what percentage of the scores are lower on the scale. For example, if a score is at the 20th percentile, that score is greater than 20 percent of the scores. The 90th percentile refers to the score which is greater than 90 percent of the other scores.

For most exercises in this workbook, percentile ranks will be computed because they are easy to compute. (There are other methods described in the suggested readings.) *Percentile ranks* are approximations of percentiles and will suffice to illustrate measurement principles.

Percentile ranks are computed in the following way:

1. Design a table for the computations like the one illustrated in Figure 1.1, and list the possible test scores from low to high.
2. In the frequency column, record the number of people scoring at each level.
3. Tabulate these scores by writing down the ranks of the scores from the low to high scores.
4. The *average rank* is the average of the numbers in that raw score category.
5. Divide the average rank by the total number of cases to find the percentile rank.

IGAT NORMS

In this exercise, percentile ranks are computed for each subtest of the IGAT. Data should be gathered from the class and recorded in Tables 2.1–2.8. In the frequency column, record the number of people scoring at each level. Tabulate these scores by writing down the ranks of the scores from low to high scores. Compute the average rank and percentile rank in the manner described and illustrated previously.

The percentile ranks show the percentage of the group that scored at or below each raw score. The separate norms for each subtest allow the examiner to compare the subject's score with the scores of the other subjects on that particular subtest. It will be noted that a given raw score, of say 9, has different meanings depending on the subtest involved. It will be further noted that a subject may score high on one subtest and very low on another subtest. The pattern of scores for an individual is presented visually by means of the test profile.

Raw Score	Frequency	Tabulate	Average Rank	%ile Rank
.	.	.	.	.
.	.	.	.	.
.	.	.	.	.
.	.	.	.	.
7	3	6,7,8	7	35
6	2	4,5	4.5	22.5
5	1	3	3	15
4	2	1,2	1.5	7.5
Total $N = 20$				

Figure 1.1   Illustration of Computation of Percentile Ranks

PROFILES

Test profiles should be prepared for each of the subjects tested by each examiner (student) in Exercise 1. The profile sheets will be found in the laboratory materials. The steps in plotting the test profile are as follows:

1. Convert the first subtest raw score to a percentile by using the norm tables you have constructed.
2. Enter the percentile in the blank space under the subtest initial (I for Information, etc.).
3. Mark the percentile on the profile.
4. Draw a straight line connecting the marks on adjacent subtests.

The next step is to compute a total verbal, a total nonverbal, and an overall total score. Since percentile scores are not equal units of measure, they cannot be averaged. In order to average the scores, they must first be converted to standard scores. For this exercise, we will use T scores which have a mean of 50 and standard deviation of 10. After the mean standard score is obtained, it can be converted back to a percentile score. The specific steps in this procedure are as follows:

1. Look up the T score corresponding to the subtest percentile. The following conversion table provides a conversion from percentile to standard scores or vice versa. Specific scores not listed can be approximated by interpolation.
2. Enter the T score below the profile of the subtest.
3. Repeat the procedure for the next subtest.
4. Add the four T scores for the verbal section (I, A, V, M), and divide by 4 to obtain the mean verbal T score.
5. Enter the mean verbal T score in the space provided.
6. Read the percentile corresponding to the T score from the conversion table and enter it in the space provided.
7. Repeat the procedure for the nonverbal tests (N, S, O, L).
8. Add the mean vebal T score and the mean nonverbal T score and divide by 2 to obtain the mean total T score.
9. Enter the corresponding percentile in the space marked "Total."

Conversion Table

%ile	Standard Score	%ile	Standard Score
99	72	50	50
98	70	42	48
96	68	34	46
94	66	28	44
92	64	21	42
88	62	16	40
84	60	11	38
79	58	8	36
73	56	6	34
66	54	4	32
58	52	2	30
50	50	1	28

Note: The standard scores in this table are T scores and have a mean of 50 and standard deviation of 10.

INTERPRETATION OF PROFILES

People who have the same overall level of general problem-solving ability can still be very different from each other in the kinds of problems that they solve well. This is why a wide variety of different kinds of items are usually used when testing for general ability. It gives the person who is weak in one area a chance to compensate by doing well with other kinds of problems or questions. The *overall score,* then, is an average that represents how well a person is likely to do, generally, when faced with a range of different kinds of problems.

But the overall score does not show anything about the differences in problem-solving abilities within a person, that is, that person's strengths and weaknesses. The test profile offers an opportunity to do that. With some kinds of general ability tests, the examiner can look at the profile and suggest some hypotheses about the person based on the relative levels of the different subscores. This is possible by examining the differences in scores on separate parts of the test and noting the patterns of highs and lows.

Each of the subtests is planned to measure a somewhat different facet of general ability. With a real test of this type, the examiner will have reviewed and discussed studies that show how different patterns of test scores relate to different abilities, and will have at least a fairly good basis for interpreting the profile. In this laboratory exercise, we are using a test that is similar to the usual individually administered general ability tests. However, we do not have the years of research on test patterns that would be available to the professional examiner using a real test. In order to do a profile analysis, therefore, we will assign meanings to the subscales based on how they were constructed, what kind of problem-solving ability they were designed to measure, and what they appear to measure. Any profile interpretations must be viewed as very tentative. They are only hypotheses or suggestions that need to be checked out further before assuming they are true.

The same kind of caution would be used in doing a profile interpretation with a real and well-validated test. You would be able to be a little more confident of your statements about a person's strengths or weaknesses, but would always have to view them as tentative hypotheses that need further confirmation. One reason is that subscales on a test like this may not be very reliable. The total test is quite long, and a small error, a misscoring, or a poor item, will not have much effect on the total score. Each subscale, however, is quite short. Even a small accidental error could change the score quite a bit. Added to this is that the *differences* between subscales, which is what we are looking at when we interpret a profile, may be even less reliable than the subscales themselves.

Despite these problems, as long as the examiner treats the hypotheses with caution, they can be useful. Hypotheses suggest ideas that can be checked out further, either by looking at other information about the person or by discussing them in a counseling session with a professional counselor.

DESCRIPTIONS OF SUBSCALES

Remember that the following descriptions are based on what the subscales should logically measure.

Verbal and Nonverbal Scales

The subscales are divided into two groups: scales that require verbal facility and those that do not. A large difference between the verbal and nonverbal scores could indicate a difference in basic problem-solving style. High verbal scores and low nonverbal scores could suggest a person who attempts to analyze everything in terms of words. This might go along with a low interest in sciences and/or mathematics. A low verbal and high nonverbal pattern of scores may indicate a deficit in language skills, which might be experienced by a person reared in a culturally different environment (or a foreign country).

Information

Each of the items on the information scale is designed to be relatively easy for a person who has some background in the general area. The items taken together would indicate the range of knowledge that a person possesses. A high information score, then, would suggest a wide range of interests. It might relate to a background where parents or relatives were highly educated and discussed things with or in front of children. A high score might mean that the person did well in school in a lot of different subjects.

A low score might suggest a person who is striving to overcome a poor educational background. It might, however, mean that the person has only a narrow range of interests and that he or she had focused on only one or two areas for some time. Another possibility is that the person has done poorly in school in some courses and well in others.

Analogies

Solving analogies probably requires seeing how things fit together. It could be related to the ability to find solutions to problems. Since, to solve an analogy problem, you sometimes have to try various meanings and solutions until you find one that works, the person scoring well on this test might have to be more flexible in the way he or she approaches problems.

A low score could suggest that the person would have trouble with some kinds of problems, particularly those that require trying different solutions until the right one is found.

Vocabulary

Vocabulary is often a good general measure of the ability to learn. The vocabulary score is likely to be more highly correlated with the total score on a general ability test than any of the other subscales. If there is a high vocabulary score and a lower score on another of the verbal scales, the vocabulary score might indicate the level that could be expected on the other score, suggesting that the other score is lower than it ought to be. You might ask yourself "Why is it lower?" and state hypotheses about that.

A *very* high vocabulary score might indicate that the person does quite a bit of reading or that the family members are highly educated. A low score could mean a lower general ability to learn and that the person might have trouble in college. It could, however, be an indication that the person had a low level of exposure to these words. There could be a different cultural or language background or a real lack of interest in verbal areas. Remember that a low score on any subscale is only low for the group that volunteered to take the test. A "low" vocabulary score, therefore, may still be fairly good when considered among all college students and might not indicate any real problems.

Letter Memory

The letter memory test is planned to measure short-term memory. A good score on this test might require the ability to concentrate and pick up information accurately, as, for example, from a lecture. The person might be good at listening to lectures and taking accurate notes. A *very* high score may also suggest another ability. The person who gets a very high score usually organizes the task mentally and breaks up the letters into shorter groups, remembering and repeating the groups. The very high score could indicate an ability to rapidly organize a mental task.

A low score could suggest that the person has some trouble because of distractions or difficulty concentrating. The person might not be able to "tune out" outside noise or activity while studying. Another possibility, if the person had a very low score, is that the person could be anxious while taking tests, and outside thoughts related to the anxiety might be interfering with concentration and short-term memory.

Number Series

The number series items are planned to assess the ability to see relationships among numbers. It might be related to the ability to find solutions to problems in mathematics or possibly in science problems. A large difference between this test and the Analogies test might indicate a strong differential ability between problem solving that involves verbal concepts and problem solving that involves math.

A low score might be related to poor potential in mathematics. It could also relate to high mathematics anxiety, preventing the person from being able to work on the problems.

Spatial Relations

The paper-tearing test is planned to look at the way a person thinks about sizes and shapes. To get a high score, the person should be able to see the size of the piece that is to be torn off as an organized part of the shape and size of the whole sheet of paper. On the clock test, the person has to be able to visualize a complex object from another direction or point of view. A high score might relate to the ability to see and handle shapes and sizes and fit them into spaces. It could be important in solving problems or doing tasks in geometry, construction, drawing, or possibly even in games like chess.

A low score could suggest difficulty in any task that involves judging or handling size and shape. The person with a low score could find any of the previous subjects difficult. The person might even have trouble learning how to back up a car or putting packages in a cupboard.

Object Relations

A person with some knowledge of physical science, for example, the orbital relationships of the sun, earth, and moon system, would probably score well on this subtest. This knowledge should be associated with a general curiosity about physical things and how they work. A high score might also indicate that the person has the ability to see objects from different angles or points of view, a skill that might also be measured by the clock test. A high score, therefore, might be related to good spatial visualization. The person might be good in science or mechanical activities.

A low score could indicate a problem in spatial visualization. The results of the clock test and the spatial relations test might indicate whether that was true. A low score could also mean lack of interest in or knowledge of physical science principles.

Sign Language

The sign language subscale is the most complex scale to try to interpret on a profile. There are several different possibilities that could lead to a high score. You will need to consider what else you know about the person to help you decide what a high score means. First, the high score could result from a very high ability to recognize, remember, and compare simple figures. Second, each figure can be logically related to its meaning. Third, each line is a sentence, so the person who is sensitive to language structure can gain time because that person can look quickly for appropriate nouns, verbs, and objects. Fourth, the story is a reasonable one. The person who sees a developing situation as a logical story could gain time.

The way a person takes this test may reveal whether a high score resulted only from recognizing and comparing figures rapidly. If you observed carefully, you might have seen the examinee make direct comparisons. The examinee might have read the story word by word, such as "boy, girl, see, deer, deer." Watching how the person reads the sentences might tell you whether the figures were logically related to the words. Did the examinee quickly learn some figures and not have to look them up? Did the examinee correct errors by checking differences or saying something like "Oh, antlers, that is deer, not horse?" These kinds of observations are a very important part of test administration and can help greatly in suggesting hypotheses about the person.

If the score seems related almost entirely to recognition and comparison, a high score can suggest high energy, quick responses, and possibly a person who is highly motivated to do well on tests. A low score might be due to poor pattern recognition that could also have caused early problems in learning to read. It could merely mean the person was not trying hard on the test.

A very high score might also suggest good basic awareness of language structure and might be slightly related to a good social perception. A low score might indicate low levels in either of these areas. Again, observation of the person while taking the test might help in interpreting it. Did the person use complete sentences for each line, or did the mistakes make the sentences incomplete? Did the person seem to be guessing at what the story would say?

DIRECTIONS FOR INTERPRETING AN IGAT PROFILE

1. First, examine the overall level of the profile. Is it generally high or low? What would that mean in terms of general ability if this test were an accurate predictor of general ability to solve problems?

2. Next, check the level of the verbal and the nonverbal scores. Is there a large difference? What could that difference mean?
3. Note the high and low scales. What would a high score or a low score on a particular scale suggest?
4. Note combinations of high and low scales. The combination can sometimes suggest more than each scale alone. (For examples, see the next section.)
5. Integrate the suggestions about the person that came from the test with other information about the person. Does other information tend to confirm ideas from the test? Does it contradict?
6. Write suggestions about the person based on the profile analysis at the bottom of the profile sheet. Use a qualifying phrase with each suggestion, such as "This person may . . ." or "There could be . . ." or a similar phrase that shows the statement is tentative.

EXAMPLES OF INTERPRETATIONS
OF COMBINATIONS OF SCORES

If you can, try to combine the information about two or more subscales into a hypothesis that takes both subscales into account as shown in the following four examples. This takes some ingenuity, but it can be done by the best professional examiners. When you know something about the person's background that might help explain a difference, add a comment about it. The following are examples of statements about subscale scores that might be found in a test interpretation:

1. The high vocabulary and low general information suggests that she might have a good general ability to learn but a limited range of interests. For example, she wants to be a musician and has few other interests.
2. The nonverbal scores are well below the verbal scores, and among the verbal scores, the information test is also low. He missed most of the science types of items on the information test. He may have low science and mechanical abilities and interests. However, the person is planning to major in engineering. Hence, the test results suggest that he may have difficulty in that major and might do better in a more verbally oriented field.
3. All scores are relatively high except for the sign language test. She worked very slowly, checking back and forth for each sign, and never seemed to catch on to the story. She has good social and language skills and has a high civil service rating as a secretary, so she should have done better on the test. She might have simply felt that accuracy was the most important part of the test and worked more slowly than necessary.
4. There are high scores on vocabulary and information, but he had a very low score on analogies. He could have a very good general level of ability to learn, but have difficulty solving problems that involve trying various solutions. He might get stuck on an approach to a problem and not be able to find a new one easily.

SUGGESTED READINGS

Anastasi, A. *Psychological Testing* (4th ed.). New York: Macmillan, 1976, pp. 67–102.
Brown, F. G. *Principles of Educational and Psychological Testing* (2nd ed.). New York: Holt, Rinehart and Winston, 1976, pp. 174–201.
Cronbach, L. J. *Essentials of Psychological Testing* (3rd ed.). New York: Harper & Row, 1970, pp. 82–113.
Gronlund, N. E. *Measurement and Evaluation in Teaching* (3rd ed.). New York: Macmillan, 1976, pp. 387–424.
Mehrens, W. A., and Lehmann, I. J. *Measurement and Evaluation in Education and Psychology* (2nd ed.). New York: Holt, Rinehart and Winston, 1975, pp. 133–156.
Thorndike, R. L., and Hagen, E. *Measurement and Evaluation in Psychology and Education* (4th ed.). New York: Wiley, 1977, pp. 113–149.

Table 2.1 Information

Raw Score	Frequency	Tabulate	Average Rank	%ile Rank
12				
11				
10				
9				
8				
7				
6				
5				
4				
3				
2				
1				
0				

Table 2.2 Analogies

Raw Score	Frequency	Tabulate	Average Rank	%ile Rank
8				
7				
6				
5				
4				
3				
2				
1				
0				

Table 2.3 Vocabulary

Raw Score	Frequency	Tabulate	Average Rank	%ile Rank
10				
9				
8				
7				
6				
5				
4				
3				
2				
1				
0				

Table 2.4 Letter Memory

Raw Score	Frequency	Tabulate	Average Rank	%ile Rank
10				
9				
8				
7				
6				
5				
4				
3				
2				
1				
0				

Table 2.5 Number Series

Raw Score	Frequency	Tabulate	Average Rank	%ile Rank
8				
7				
6				
5				
4				
3				
2				
1				
0				

Table 2.6 Spatial Relations

Raw Score	Frequency	Tabulate	Average Rank	%ile Rank
14				
13				
12				
11				
10				
9				
8				
7				
6				
5				
4				
3				
2				
1				
0				

Table 2.7 Object Relations

Raw Score	Frequency	Tabulate	Average Rank	%ile Rank
8				
7				
6				
5				
4				
3				
2				
1				
0				

Table 2.8 Sign Language

Raw Score	Frequency	Tabulate	Average Rank	%ile Rank
12				
11				
10				
9				
8				
7				
6				
5				
4				
3				
2				
1				
0				

Name _____

IGAT Profile

Examinee _____ Age _____ Sex _____ College Year _____ GPA _____

%ile	I	A	V	M	Total Verbal	%ile	N	S	O	L	Total Non-verbal	Total
99						99						
98						98						
96						96						
94						94						
92						92						
88						88						
84						84						
79						79						
73						73						
66						66						
58						58						
50						50						
42						42						
34						34						
28						28						
21						21						
16						16						
11						11						
8						8						
6						6						
4						4						
2						2						
1						1						

Raw Score ____

Percentile ____

T Score ____

Mean Verbal T Score ____   Mean Verbal Total T Score ____   Mean Verbal T Score ____   Mean Total T Score ____   Mean Total T Score ____

37

Name _____

IGAT Profile

Examinee _____

Age _____ Sex _____ College Year _____ GPA _____

%ile	I	A	V	M	Total Verbal	%ile	N	S	O	L	Total Non-verbal	Total
99						99						
98						98						
96						96						
94						94						
92						92						
88						88						
84						84						
79						79						
73						73						
66						66						
58						58						
50						50						
42						42						
34						34						
28						28						
21						21						
16						16						
11						11						
8						8						
6						6						
4						4						
2						2						
1						1						

Raw Score _____

Percentile _____

T Score _____

Mean Verbal T Score _____

Mean Verbal Total T Score _____

Mean Total T Score _____

Name _____

IGAT Profile

Examinee _____ Age _____ Sex _____ College Year _____ GPA _____

%ile	I	A	V	M	Total Verbal	%ile	N	S	O	L	Total Non-verbal	Total
99						99						
98						98						
96						96						
94						9.						
92						92						
88						88						
84						84						
79						79						
73						73						
66						66						
58						58						
50						50						
42						42						
34						34						
28						28						
21						21						
16						16						
11						11						
8						8						
6						6						
4						4						
2						2						
1						1						

Raw Score _____

Percentile _____

T Score _____

Mean Verbal T Score _____

Mean Total T Score _____

Name _____

IGAT Profile

Examinee _____ Age _____ Sex _____ College Year _____ GPA _____

%ile	I	A	V	M	Total Verbal	%ile	N	S	O	L	Total Non-verbal	Total
99						99						
98						98						
96						96						
94						94						
92						92						
88						88						
84						84						
79						79						
73						73						
66						66						
58						58						
50						50						
42						42						
34						34						
28						28						
21						21						
16						16						
11						11						
8						8						
6						6						
4						4						
2						2						
1						1						

Raw Score ____ ____ ____ ____ ____ ____ ____ ____ ____ ____

Percentile ____ ____ ____ ____ ____

T Score ____ ____ ____ ____ ____

Mean Verbal T Score ____

Mean Verbal T Score ____

Mean Total T Score ____

IGAT Profile

Examinee _____ Age ____ Sex ____ College Year ____ GPA ____

%ile	I	A	V	M	Total Verbal	%ile	N	S	O	L	Total Non-verbal	Total
99						99						
98						98						
96						96						
94						94						
92						92						
88						88						
84						84						
79						79						
73						73						
66						66						
58						58						
50						50						
42						42						
34						34						
28						28						
21						21						
16						16						
11						11						
8						8						
6						6						
4						4						
2						2						
1						1						

Raw Score ____ ____ ____ ____ ____ ____

Percentile ____ ____ ____ ____ ____ ____

T Score ____ ____ ____ ____ ____ ____

Mean Verbal T Score ____

Mean Non-verbal T Score ____

Mean Verbal T Score ____

Mean Total T Score ____

Assignment for **EXERCISE 2**

1. Complete the norm tables by computing the percentile ranks for the raw scores on the eight subtests of the IGAT.
2. Convert the raw scores into percentiles, and prepare a test profile sheet for each person you examined. Calculate and profile average scores for verbal, nonverbal, and total scores.
3. Discuss the test results with the people you examined.
4. Answer the following questions:
   a. What are the characteristics of a good norm group? What biases may be in your norm group?

   b. What are the advantages of expressing norms in terms of percentiles? What are the advantages of standard scores?

   c. What difficulties, if any, did you have in discussing the results with examinees? What did you learn from the experience?

   d. What characteristics must the subscores of this (or any) test possess if we wish to do interpretations of the *patterns* in the profile?

Group General Ability Test

This is a test of your general mental ability. Each problem is followed by several answers. Write the *letter* of the correct answer in the space provided.

1. The nationality of Beethoven was

    (a) English   (b) French   (c) German   (d) Austrian   _____

2. The composer of "An American in Paris" was

    (a) Bernstein   (b) Stokowsky   (c) Gershwin   (d) Kelly   _____

3. The author of the play on which *My Fair Lady* is based is

    (a) Goldsmith   (b) Shaw   (c) Fitzgerald   (d) Baldwin   _____

4. The 1812 Overture was written about

    (a) Commodore Perry   (b) Lone Ranger   (c) Napoleon   (d) Andrew Jackson   _____

5. Chittlins should be cooked

    (a) 3 minutes   (b) 30 minutes   (c) 1-2 hours   (d) 4-5 hours   _____

6. The formula $C_{12}H_{22}O_{11}$ stands for

    (a) Carbonic acid   (b) Alcohol   (c) Sugar   (d) Quinine   _____

7. The record for running the mile is about

    (a) 3:37   (b) 3:55   (c) 4:01   (d) 4:45   _____

8. The distance between the bases in baseball is

    (a) 75 feet   (b) 90 feet   (c) 100 feet   (d) 150 feet   _____

9. The heaviest president of the United States was

    (a) Theodore Roosevelt   (b) A. Johnson   (c) Jefferson   (d) Taft   _____

10. The Fourteenth Amendment to the U.S. Constitution was passed under

    (a) Lincoln   (b) A. Johnson   (c) Jefferson   (d) McKinley   _____

11. *A Tale of Two Cities* was written by

    (a) Defoe   (b) Sade   (c) Dickens   (d) Poe   _____

12. *Arrowsmith* was written by

    (a) Babbitt   (b) Lewis   (c) Hawthorne   (d) James   _____

13. The author of *Soul on Ice* is

    (a) Baldwin   (b) Haley   (c) Cleaver   (d) Parks   _____

14. *Leaves of Grass* was written by

    (a) Whittier   (b) Sandburg   (c) Whitman   (d) Thoreau   _____

15. Airplane is to wing as car is to

    (a) Motor   (b) Hood   (c) Wheels   (d) Person   _____

16. World War II is to Hitler as World War I is to

    (a) Bismarck   (b) Roosevelt   (c) Wilhelm   (d) Churchill   _____

17. Singer is to aria as actor is to

    (a) Scene   (b) Script   (c) Soliloquy   (d) Dialogue   _____

18. Heart is to aorta as pump is to

    (a) Valve   (b) Ventricle   (c) Chamber   (d) Pipeline   ———

19. B flat is to D as E is to

    (a) G   (b) F sharp   (c) F   (d) G sharp   ———

20. Straight line is to curve as $4x + 3y = 10$ is to

    (a) $4x + 8 = 12$ (b) $x^2 = 8$ (c) $3x^2 + 12y = 8$ (d) $x - y = 9$ ———

21. Comprehend means the same as

    (a) Understand   (b) Describe   (c) Determine   (d) Construct   ———

22. Redundant means the same as

    (a) Loud   (b) Superfluous   (c) Ignorant   (d) Devious   ———

23. Arbitrary means the same as

    (a) Decision   (b) Refer   (c) Argue   (d) Discretionary   ———

24. A hog means the same as

    (a) Car   (b) Bus   (c) Taxi   (d) Bike   ———

25. Salacious means the same as

    (a) Tenacious   (b) Salty   (c) Lustful   (d) Significant   ———

26. Epistle means the same as

    (a) Saint   (b) Letter   (c) Plant   (d) Religion   ———

27. APRSOV

    How many of the following sets of letters are exactly like the above example?

    APRSVO   ARPSVO   APRSOV
      APRSOV   ASPRVO   ARSPOV

    (a) One   (b) Two   (c) Three   (d) Four   ———

28. QMNDTSW

    How many of the following sets of letters are exactly like the above example?

    QNMDTSW   QMNTDSW   QMNDTSW
      QMNTSDW   QMNDTSW   QMNDTSW

    (a) One   (b) Two   (c) Three   (d) Four   ———

29. LBKMRSVO

    How many of the following sets of letters are exactly like the above example?

    LBKMRSVO   LKBRMSVO   LBKMSRVO
      LBKRMSVO   LBKMVSOR   LBMKRSVO

    (a) One   (b) Two   (c) Three   (d) Four   ———

30. KPZBLQRTVWN

    How many of the following sets of letters are exactly like the above example?

    KPZBLQRTWVN   KPZLBQRTVWN   KPZBLQRTVWN
      KPZBQRTVWN   KPZBLQTRVWN
    KPZBLQRTVWN   KPZBLQRVTWN

    (a) One   (b) Two   (c) Three   (d) Four   ———

31. Which of the following numbers belongs with these numbers 5, 7, 19, 22?

    (a) 4   (b) 6   (c) 14   (d) 13   ———

32. Which of the following numbers belongs with these numbers 9, 9, 27, 81?

    (a) 400   (b) 327   (c) 57   (d) 729   ———

33. Which of the following numbers completes the series 4, 12, 6, 18?

    (a) 8   (b) 9   (c) 36   (d) 10   _____

34. Which of the following numbers completes the series 1, 2, 5, 26?

    (a) 37   (b) 47   (c) 97   (d) 677   _____

35. If the first three pieces were put together, which figure would they look like?

    (a)   (b)   (c)   _____

36. If the first four pieces were put together, which figure would they look like?

    (a)   (b)   (c)   (d)   _____

37. The circle is the size of a

    (a) Penny   (b) Nickel   (c) Dime   (d) Quarter

    _____

38. Which of the following lines is the width of a dollar bill?

    (a)

    (b)

    (c)

    (d)

    _____

39. Draw a 3-pound weight, a 1-pound weight, and a ½-pound weight on the balance below so that they balance.

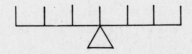

_____

40. Draw a human eye in this space.

41. Write the third letter of the Greek alphabet in this space_____.

42. What does the following stand for?

      CCCP

_____

Total Score _____
Half A _____
Half B _____

Group General Ability Test

This is a test of your general mental ability. Each problem is followed by several answers. Write the *letter* of the correct answer in the space provided.

1. The nationality of Beethoven was
   (a) English   (b) French   (c) German   (d) Austrian   _____

2. The composer of "An American in Paris" was
   (a) Bernstein   (b) Stokowsky   (c) Gershwin   (d) Kelly   _____

3. The author of the play on which *My Fair Lady* is based is
   (a) Goldsmith   (b) Shaw   (c) Fitzgerald   (d) Baldwin   _____

4. The 1812 Overture was written about
   (a) Commodore Perry   (b) Lone Ranger   (c) Napoleon   (d) Andrew Jackson   _____

5. Chittlins should be cooked
   (a) 3 minutes   (b) 30 minutes   (c) 1-2 hours   (d) 4-5 hours   _____

6. The formula $C_{12}H_{22}O_{11}$ stands for
   (a) Carbonic acid   (b) Alcohol   (c) Sugar   (d) Quinine   _____

7. The record for running the mile is about
   (a) 3:37   (b) 3:55   (c) 4:01   (d) 4:45   _____

8. The distance between the bases in baseball is
   (a) 75 feet   (b) 90 feet   (c) 100 feet   (d) 150 feet   _____

9. The heaviest president of the United States was
   (a) Theodore Roosevelt   (b) A. Johnson   (c) Jefferson   (d) Taft   _____

10. The Fourteenth Amendment to the U.S. Constitution was passed under
    (a) Lincoln   (b) A. Johnson   (c) Jefferson   (d) McKinley   _____

11. *A Tale of Two Cities* was written by
    (a) Defoe   (b) Sade   (c) Dickens   (d) Poe   _____

12. *Arrowsmith* was written by
    (a) Babbitt   (b) Lewis   (c) Hawthorne   (d) James   _____

13. The author of *Soul on Ice* is
    (a) Baldwin   (b) Haley   (c) Cleaver   (d) Parks   _____

14. *Leaves of Grass* was written by
    (a) Whittier   (b) Sandburg   (c) Whitman   (d) Thoreau   _____

15. Airplane is to wing as car is to
    (a) Motor   (b) Hood   (c) Wheels   (d) Person   _____

16. World War II is to Hitler as World War I is to
    (a) Bismarck   (b) Roosevelt   (c) Wilhelm   (d) Churchill   _____

17. Singer is to aria as actor is to
    (a) Scene   (b) Script   (c) Soliloquy   (d) Dialogue   _____

18. Heart is to aorta as pump is to

    (a) Valve   (b) Ventricle   (c) Chamber   (d) Pipeline   _____

19. B flat is to D as E is to

    (a) G   (b) F sharp   (c) F   (d) G sharp   _____

20. Straight line is to curve as $4x + 3y = 10$ is to

    (a) $4x + 8 = 12$ (b) $x^2 = 8$ (c) $3x^2 + 12y = 8$ (d) $x - y = 9$ _____

21. Comprehend means the same as

    (a) Understand   (b) Describe   (c) Determine   (d) Construct   _____

22. Redundant means the same as

    (a) Loud   (b) Superfluous   (c) Ignorant   (d) Devious   _____

23. Arbitrary means the same as

    (a) Decision   (b) Refer   (c) Argue   (d) Discretionary   _____

24. A hog means the same as

    (a) Car   (b) Bus   (c) Taxi   (d) Bike   _____

25. Salacious means the same as

    (a) Tenacious   (b) Salty   (c) Lustful   (d) Significant   _____

26. Epistle means the same as

    (a) Saint   (b) Letter   (c) Plant   (d) Religion   _____

27. APRSOV

    How many of the following sets of letters are exactly like the above example?

    APRSVO   ARPSVO   APRSOV
     APRSOV   ASPRVO   ARSPOV

    (a) One   (b) Two   (c) Three   (d) Four   _____

28. QMNDTSW

    How many of the following sets of letters are exactly like the above example?

    QNMDTSW   QMNTDSW   QMNDTSW
     QMNTSDW   QMNDTSW   QMNDTSW

    (a) One   (b) Two   (c) Three   (d) Four   _____

29. LBKMRSVO

    How many of the following sets of letters are exactly like the above example?

    LBKMRSVO   LKBRMSVO   LBKMSRVO
     LBKRMSVO   LBKMVSOR   LBMKRSVO

    (a) One   (b) Two   (c) Three   (d) Four   _____

30. KPZBLQRTVWN

    How many of the following sets of letters are exactly like the above example?

    KPZBLQRTWVN   KPZLBQRTVWN   KPZBLQRTVWN
         KPZBQRTVWN   KPZBLQTRVWN
    KPZBLQRTVWN   KPZBLQRVTWN

    (a) One   (b) Two   (c) Three   (d) Four   _____

31. Which of the following numbers belongs with these numbers 5, 7, 19, 22?

    (a) 4   (b) 6   (c) 14   (d) 13   _____

32. Which of the following numbers belongs with these numbers 9, 9, 27, 81?

    (a) 400   (b) 327   (c) 57   (d) 729   _____

33. Which of the following numbers completes the series 4, 12, 6, 18?

    (a) 8   (b) 9   (c) 36   (d) 10   _____

34. Which of the following numbers completes the series 1, 2, 5, 26?

    (a) 37   (b) 47   (c) 97   (d) 677   _____

35. If the first three pieces were put together, which figure would they look like?

 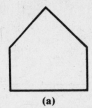 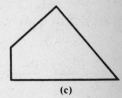

              (a)   (b)   (c)   _____

36. If the first four pieces were put together, which figure would they look like?

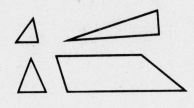 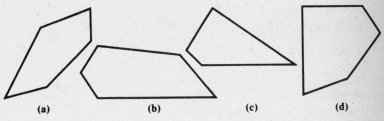

    (a)   (b)   (c)   (d)   _____

37. The circle is the size of a

    (a) Penny   (b) Nickel   (c) Dime   (d) Quarter

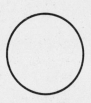

_____

38. Which of the following lines is the width of a dollar bill?

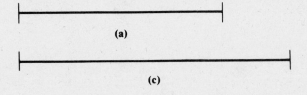 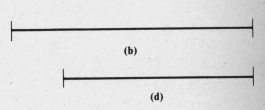

        (a)   (b)

        (c)   (d)   _____

39. Draw a 3-pound weight, a 1-pound weight, and a ½-pound weight on the balance below so that they balance.

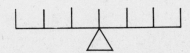

_____

40. Draw a human eye in this space.

41. Write the third letter of the Greek alphabet in this space_____.

42. What does the following stand for?

      CCCP

_____

Total Score _____
Half A _____
Half B _____

Group General Ability Test

This is a test of your general mental ability. Each problem is followed by several answers. Write the *letter* of the correct answer in the space provided.

1. The nationality of Beethoven was
   (a) English   (b) French   (c) German   (d) Austrian   _____

2. The composer of "An American in Paris" was
   (a) Bernstein   (b) Stokowsky   (c) Gershwin   (d) Kelly   _____

3. The author of the play on which *My Fair Lady* is based is
   (a) Goldsmith   (b) Shaw   (c) Fitzgerald   (d) Baldwin   _____

4. The 1812 Overture was written about
   (a) Commodore Perry   (b) Lone Ranger   (c) Napoleon   (d) Andrew Jackson   _____

5. Chittlins should be cooked
   (a) 3 minutes   (b) 30 minutes   (c) 1-2 hours   (d) 4-5 hours   _____

6. The formula $C_{12}H_{22}O_{11}$ stands for
   (a) Carbonic acid   (b) Alcohol   (c) Sugar   (d) Quinine   _____

7. The record for running the mile is about
   (a) 3:37   (b) 3:55   (c) 4:01   (d) 4:45   _____

8. The distance between the bases in baseball is
   (a) 75 feet   (b) 90 feet   (c) 100 feet   (d) 150 feet   _____

9. The heaviest president of the United States was
   (a) Theodore Roosevelt   (b) A. Johnson   (c) Jefferson   (d) Taft   _____

10. The Fourteenth Amendment to the U.S. Constitution was passed under
    (a) Lincoln   (b) A. Johnson   (c) Jefferson   (d) McKinley   _____

11. *A Tale of Two Cities* was written by
    (a) Defoe   (b) Sade   (c) Dickens   (d) Poe   _____

12. *Arrowsmith* was written by
    (a) Babbitt   (b) Lewis   (c) Hawthorne   (d) James   _____

13. The author of *Soul on Ice* is
    (a) Baldwin   (b) Haley   (c) Cleaver   (d) Parks   _____

14. *Leaves of Grass* was written by
    (a) Whittier   (b) Sandburg   (c) Whitman   (d) Thoreau   _____

15. Airplane is to wing as car is to
    (a) Motor   (b) Hood   (c) Wheels   (d) Person   _____

16. World War II is to Hitler as World War I is to
    (a) Bismarck   (b) Roosevelt   (c) Wilhelm   (d) Churchill   _____

17. Singer is to aria as actor is to
    (a) Scene   (b) Script   (c) Soliloquy   (d) Dialogue   _____

18. Heart is to aorta as pump is to

    (a) Valve   (b) Ventricle   (c) Chamber   (d) Pipeline   _____

19. B flat is to D as E is to

    (a) G   (b) F sharp   (c) F   (d) G sharp   _____

20. Straight line is to curve as $4x + 3y = 10$ is to

    (a) $4x + 8 = 12$ (b) $x^2 = 8$ (c) $3x^2 + 12y = 8$ (d) $x - y = 9$ _____

21. Comprehend means the same as

    (a) Understand   (b) Describe   (c) Determine   (d) Construct   _____

22. Redundant means the same as

    (a) Loud   (b) Superfluous   (c) Ignorant   (d) Devious   _____

23. Arbitrary means the same as

    (a) Decision   (b) Refer   (c) Argue   (d) Discretionary   _____

24. A hog means the same as

    (a) Car   (b) Bus   (c) Taxi   (d) Bike   _____

25. Salacious means the same as

    (a) Tenacious   (b) Salty   (c) Lustful   (d) Significant   _____

26. Epistle means the same as

    (a) Saint   (b) Letter   (c) Plant   (d) Religion   _____

27. APRSOV

How many of the following sets of letters are exactly like the above example?

APRSVO   ARPSVO   APRSOV
  APRSOV   ASPRVO   ARSPOV

    (a) One   (b) Two   (c) Three   (d) Four   _____

28. QMNDTSW

How many of the following sets of letters are exactly like the above example?

QNMDTSW   QMNTDSW   QMNDTSW
  QMNTSDW   QMNDTSW   QMNDTSW

    (a) One   (b) Two   (c) Three   (d) Four   _____

29. LBKMRSVO

How many of the following sets of letters are exactly like the above example?

LBKMRSVO   LKBRMSVO   LBKMSRVO
  LBKRMSVO   LBKMVSOR   LBMKRSVO

    (a) One   (b) Two   (c) Three   (d) Four   _____

30. KPZBLQRTVWN

How many of the following sets of letters are exactly like the above example?

KPZBLQRTWVN   KPZLBQRTVWN   KPZBLQRTVWN
    KPZBQRTVWN   KPZBLQTRVWN
KPZBLQRTVWN   KPZBLQRVTWN

    (a) One   (b) Two   (c) Three   (d) Four   _____

31. Which of the following numbers belongs with these numbers 5, 7, 19, 22?

    (a) 4   (b) 6   (c) 14   (d) 13   _____

32. Which of the following numbers belongs with these numbers 9, 9, 27, 81?

    (a) 400   (b) 327   (c) 57   (d) 729   _____

33. Which of the following numbers completes the series 4, 12, 6, 18?
    (a) 8   (b) 9   (c) 36   (d) 10   _____

34. Which of the following numbers completes the series 1, 2, 5, 26?
    (a) 37   (b) 47   (c) 97   (d) 677   _____

35. If the first three pieces were put together, which figure would they look like?

 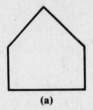 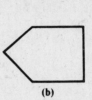 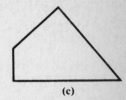

    (a)   (b)   (c)

_____

36. If the first four pieces were put together, which figure would they look like?

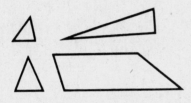 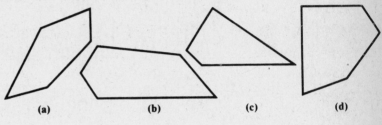

    (a)   (b)   (c)   (d)

_____

37. The circle is the size of a
    (a) Penny   (b) Nickel   (c) Dime   (d) Quarter

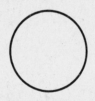

_____

38. Which of the following lines is the width of a dollar bill?

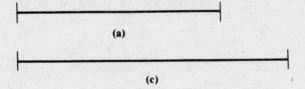 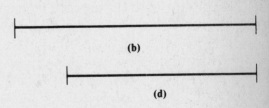

    (a)   (b)

    (c)   (d)

_____

39. Draw a 3-pound weight, a 1-pound weight, and a ½-pound weight on the balance below so that they balance.

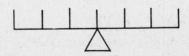

_____

40. Draw a human eye in this space.

41. Write the third letter of the Greek alphabet in this space_____.

42. What does the following stand for?

    CCCP

_____

Total Score _____
Half A _____
Half B _____

Group General Ability Test

This is a test of your general mental ability. Each problem is followed by several answers. Write the *letter* of the correct answer in the space provided.

1. The nationality of Beethoven was
   (a) English   (b) French   (c) German   (d) Austrian   _____

2. The composer of "An American in Paris" was
   (a) Bernstein   (b) Stokowsky   (c) Gershwin   (d) Kelly   _____

3. The author of the play on which *My Fair Lady* is based is
   (a) Goldsmith   (b) Shaw   (c) Fitzgerald   (d) Baldwin   _____

4. The 1812 Overture was written about
   (a) Commodore Perry   (b) Lone Ranger   (c) Napoleon   (d) Andrew Jackson   _____

5. Chittlins should be cooked
   (a) 3 minutes   (b) 30 minutes   (c) 1-2 hours   (d) 4-5 hours   _____

6. The formula $C_{12}H_{22}O_{11}$ stands for
   (a) Carbonic acid   (b) Alcohol   (c) Sugar   (d) Quinine   _____

7. The record for running the mile is about
   (a) 3:37   (b) 3:55   (c) 4:01   (d) 4:45   _____

8. The distance between the bases in baseball is
   (a) 75 feet   (b) 90 feet   (c) 100 feet   (d) 150 feet   _____

9. The heaviest president of the United States was
   (a) Theodore Roosevelt   (b) A. Johnson   (c) Jefferson   (d) Taft   _____

10. The Fourteenth Amendment to the U.S. Constitution was passed under
    (a) Lincoln   (b) A. Johnson   (c) Jefferson   (d) McKinley   _____

11. *A Tale of Two Cities* was written by
    (a) Defoe   (b) Sade   (c) Dickens   (d) Poe   _____

12. *Arrowsmith* was written by
    (a) Babbitt   (b) Lewis   (c) Hawthorne   (d) James   _____

13. The author of *Soul on Ice* is
    (a) Baldwin   (b) Haley   (c) Cleaver   (d) Parks   _____

14. *Leaves of Grass* was written by
    (a) Whittier   (b) Sandburg   (c) Whitman   (d) Thoreau   _____

15. Airplane is to wing as car is to
    (a) Motor   (b) Hood   (c) Wheels   (d) Person   _____

16. World War II is to Hitler as World War I is to
    (a) Bismarck   (b) Roosevelt   (c) Wilhelm   (d) Churchill   _____

17. Singer is to aria as actor is to
    (a) Scene   (b) Script   (c) Soliloquy   (d) Dialogue   _____

18. Heart is to aorta as pump is to

    (a) Valve   (b) Ventricle   (c) Chamber   (d) Pipeline   _____

19. B flat is to D as E is to

    (a) G   (b) F sharp   (c) F   (d) G sharp   _____

20. Straight line is to curve as $4x + 3y = 10$ is to

    (a) $4x + 8 = 12$ (b) $x^2 = 8$ (c) $3x^2 + 12y = 8$ (d) $x - y = 9$ _____

21. Comprehend means the same as

    (a) Understand   (b) Describe   (c) Determine   (d) Construct   _____

22. Redundant means the same as

    (a) Loud   (b) Superfluous   (c) Ignorant   (d) Devious   _____

23. Arbitrary means the same as

    (a) Decision   (b) Refer   (c) Argue   (d) Discretionary   _____

24. A hog means the same as

    (a) Car   (b) Bus   (c) Taxi   (d) Bike   _____

25. Salacious means the same as

    (a) Tenacious   (b) Salty   (c) Lustful   (d) Significant   _____

26. Epistle means the same as

    (a) Saint   (b) Letter   (c) Plant   (d) Religion   _____

27. APRSOV

How many of the following sets of letters are exactly like the above example?

APRSVO   ARPSVO   APRSOV
  APRSOV   ASPRVO   ARSPOV

    (a) One   (b) Two   (c) Three   (d) Four   _____

28. QMNDTSW

How many of the following sets of letters are exactly like the above example?

QNMDTSW   QMNTDSW   QMNDTSW
  QMNTSDW   QMNDTSW   QMNDTSW

    (a) One   (b) Two   (c) Three   (d) Four   _____

29. LBKMRSVO

How many of the following sets of letters are exactly like the above example?

LBKMRSVO   LKBRMSVO   LBKMSRVO
  LBKRMSVO   LBKMVSOR   LBMKRSVO

    (a) One   (b) Two   (c) Three   (d) Four   _____

30. KPZBLQRTVWN

How many of the following sets of letters are exactly like the above example?

KPZBLQRTWVN   KPZLBQRTVWN   KPZBLQRTVWN
    KPZBQRTVWN   KPZBLQTRVWN
KPZBLQRTVWN   KPZBLQRVTWN

    (a) One   (b) Two   (c) Three   (d) Four   _____

31. Which of the following numbers belongs with these numbers 5, 7, 19, 22?

    (a) 4   (b) 6   (c) 14   (d) 13   _____

32. Which of the following numbers belongs with these numbers 9, 9, 27, 81?

    (a) 400   (b) 327   (c) 57   (d) 729   _____

33. Which of the following numbers completes the series 4, 12, 6, 18?

    (a) 8   (b) 9   (c) 36   (d) 10   _____

34. Which of the following numbers completes the series 1, 2, 5, 26?

    (a) 37   (b) 47   (c) 97   (d) 677   _____

35. If the first three pieces were put together, which figure would they look like?

    (a)   (b)   (c)   _____

36. If the first four pieces were put together, which figure would they look like?

    (a)   (b)   (c)   (d)   _____

37. The circle is the size of a

    (a) Penny   (b) Nickel   (c) Dime   (d) Quarter   _____

38. Which of the following lines is the width of a dollar bill?

    (a)

    (b)

    (c)

    (d)   _____

39. Draw a 3-pound weight, a 1-pound weight, and a ½-pound weight on the balance below so that they balance.

_____

40. Draw a human eye in this space.

41. Write the third letter of the Greek alphabet in this space_____.

42. What does the following stand for?

     CCCP

_____

Total Score _____
Half A _____
Half B _____

70

Assignment for **Exercise 3**

1. Administer the GGAT to five college students.
2. Score the tests and record the total points earned on the end of the exam.
3. Answer the following questions:
    a. List four advantages of multiple-choice items in comparison with questions requiring a written response and questions given orally, such as the Individual General Ability Test (IGAT).

    b. Compare the content of GGAT and IGAT. What cognitive abilities can be tested better with each format?

    c. What problems, if any, did you encounter when administering the GGAT? What did you learn from the experience?

Reliability:
Internal Consistency
of the GGAT

INTRODUCTION

This exercise illustrates two methods of estimating the reliability of a test. Both methods provide an indication of the internal consistency of the test and the adequacy of the sample of item content in the test. First, the GGAT is divided into two halves, and a correlation of the scores on these two halves is computed. When this correlation coefficient is corrected, it gives one indication of the reliability of the test. Second, the Kuder-Richardson Formula 20 (KR_{20}) is computed using information about individual test items.

RELIABILITY

Reliability is defined as the accuracy of measurement of a test. Accuracy in this context has two related, yet somewhat different, meanings: (1) *consistency,* the extent to which different parts of the test or different forms of the test measure the same thing, and (2) *stability,* the extent to which the test measures the same thing at different times or in different situations. In measurement terminology, we say a test is reliable if the scores are free from random errors of measurement. This definition is built on the concept that a person's test score is composed of part "true" score and part "error" score. If there is much random error affecting the test score, the test can not measure accurately. Of course, there are many different types of factors which might affect test scores.

Procedures for estimating reliability give an indication of the extent to which different types of potential errors of measurement actually affect test scores. Stability of measurement is estimated by correlating the scores on the test given at one time with the scores on the same test at a later time. This correlation is often called the *coefficient of stability;* as a "test-retest" estimate, it indicates whether time-related errors affect the scores. Consistency of measurement is estimated in one of several ways. Scores on two halves of the test can be correlated with each other. This correlation, often called the *split-half coefficient,* indicates the effects of errors due to sampling of item content. Other internal consistency procedures, including KR_{20} and coefficient alpha, involve analysis of information for all individual items on a test. These procedures indicate adequacy of content sampling and the extent to which the content on the test measures a single, homogeneous construct. Still another way to check the adequacy of content sampling is to correlate the scores on two equivalent forms of the test. This correlation, called the *coefficient of equivalence,* is an indication of the extent to which the test is an adequate sample of items which have been put on the test.

SPLIT-HALF RELIABILITY

In Exercise 3, each member of the class administered the GGAT to 5 people. In this exercise, you will use 20 of those people for the reliability studies. Your instructor will specify how you will select among your examinees.

If there are 20 students in your class, you might randomly select one GGAT from each student.

The test is divided into halves by finding each individual's score on the "odd-numbered" items and "even-numbered" items. The two scores for each subject are recorded in Table 4.1, and the rank-order correlation between the two sets of scores is computed.

The rank-order correlation is a simple method of computing a measure of relationship. If the student is not familiar with the procedure, the instructor may ask the student to complete a supplementary exercise in Laboratory Exercise C.

RANK-ORDER CORRELATION PROCEDURE:

1. Rank order the scores for the "odd-numbered items." Give the lowest score a rank of "1," and record this in the column headed "Subjects' Rank on Odds." Give ranks from "2" to "20" to the other scores.
2. Rank order the scores for the "even-numbered items."
3. Compute the difference (d) between these two ranks.
4. Square each of these d's, and record in the last column.
5. Find the sum of these d^2's.
6. Complete the formula, where N = the number of subjects.

Since the test has been divided into two halves to compute the correlation, the coefficient is an estimate of reliability for a test one-half the length of the original one. Reliability is partially a function of test length. The longer the test is, the more reliable it will be because errors of measurement (e.g., a momentary lapsed memory) will have less effect on the test scores. In addition, a longer test can usually cover a more representative sample of the domain being measured. Therefore, a correction must be made to obtain a better estimate of the test reliability. The correction is made with the use of the Spearman Brown prophecy formula:

$$r_n = \frac{nr}{1 + (n - 1)r}$$

Where r_n is the reliability of a test n times as long, r is the obtained correlation or reliability of the shorter test, and n is the number of times the test is lengthened.

The next step is to estimate the reliability of the test if it were doubled in length, that is, from 42 to 84 items. This is done by applying the Spearman-Brown formula with $n = 2$ again.

When a test is to be doubled in length, the formula becomes

$$r_n = \frac{2r}{1 + r}$$

KUDER-RICHARDSON FORMULA 20

To estimate the reliability of the GGAT using the KR_{20} procedure, use the following formula:

$$KR_{20} = \left(\frac{K}{K - 1}\right)\left(\frac{s_T^2 - \Sigma pq}{s_T^2}\right)$$

where

K = the number of items
s_T^2 = variance of the total test scores
p = proportion of examinees passing each item
$q = 1 - p$

Thus, you will need to know the variance of the total test and the difficulty level of each individual item.

The variance of the total test scores can be computed in Table 4.2. If you are not familiar with the computation of the standard deviation and variance, the instructor may ask you to complete supplementary exercises in Laboratory Exercise B.

In Table 4.2, record the total score on the GGAT for 20 students selected earlier. Each of these scores should be squared (X^2) and summed (ΣX^2). The formula for the variance is listed below:

$$s_T^2 = \frac{\Sigma X^2}{n} - \overline{X}^2$$

where

s_T^2 = variance of the total test

ΣX^2 = sum of the squares of the individual scores

$\overline{X}^2$ = the square of the test mean

Next, the item statistics are computed in Table 4.3:

1. Record the proportion of examinees passing each item in the first column.
2. Subtract each proportion from 1.00 and record in Column 2.
3. Multiply $p \times q$.
4. Find the sum of the pq's.
5. Complete the KR_{20} formula.

SUGGESTED READINGS

Anastasi, A. *Psychological Testing* (4th ed.). New York: Macmillan, 1976, pp. 103–133.

Brown, F. G. *Principles of Educational and Psychological Testing* (2nd ed.). New York: Holt, Rinehart and Winston, 1976, pp. 51–62, 67–96.

Cronbach, L. J. *Essentials of Psychological Testing* (3rd ed.). New York: Harper & Row, 1970, pp. 151–179.

Gronlund, N. E. *Measurement and Evaluation in Teaching* (3rd ed.). New York: Macmillan, 1976, pp. 105–125.

Mehrens, W. A., and Lehmann, I. J. *Measurement and Evaluation in Education and Psychology* (2nd ed.). New York: Holt, Rinehart and Winston, 1975, pp. 87–103.

Thorndike, R. L., and Hagan, E. *Measurement and Evaluation in Psychology and Education* (4th ed.). New York: Wiley, 1977, pp. 73–94.

Table 4.1 Computation of Split-Half Reliability for GGAT

Subjects	Score on Odd Items	Score on Even Items	Subjects' Rank on Odds	Subjects' Rank on Evens	d	d^2
A						
B						
C						
D						
E						
F						
G						
H						
I						
J						
K						
L						
M						
N						
O						
P						
Q						
R						
S						
T						

$$\Sigma d^2 = \text{_____}$$

1. Compute the odd-even reliability (where $r_{1/2\,1/2}$ = reliability for a test one-half as long as the original test):

$$r_{1/2\,1/2} = 1.00 - \left(\frac{6\Sigma d^2}{N^3 - N} \right)$$

2. Estimate the reliability of the test for its original length (r_{11}). The Spearman-Brown formula for corrected reliability is:

$$r_{11} = \frac{2\,r_{1/2\,1/2}}{1 + r_{1/2\,1/2}}$$

3. What would be the estimated reliability if the entire test were doubled in length (r_{22})?

$$r_{22} = \frac{2r_{11}}{1 + r_{11}}$$

Table 4.2 Computation of Test Variance

Student	Total Test Score for GGAT (X)	X^2
1		
2		
3		
4		
5		
6		
7		
8		
9		
10		
11		
12		
13		
14		
15		
16		
17		
18		
19		
20		

$$\Sigma X = \qquad\qquad\qquad \Sigma X^2 =$$

$$\overline{X} =$$
$$s_T^2 = \frac{\Sigma X^2}{n} - \overline{X}^2$$

Table 4.3 Computation of KR_{20}

Item	p Proportion Passing Item	q Proportion Not Passing Item	pq
1			
2			
3			
4			
5			
6			
7			
8			
9			
10			
11			
12			
13			
14			
15			
16			
17			
18			
19			
20			
21			
22			
23			
24			
25			
26			
27			
28			
29			
30			
31			
32			
33			
34			
35			
36			
37			
38			
39			
40			
41			
42			

$$\Sigma pq = \underline{\hspace{1cm}}$$

$$KR_{20} \text{ reliability} = \left(\frac{K}{K-1}\right)\left(\frac{s_T^2 - \Sigma pq}{s_T^2}\right)$$

Assignment for **EXERCISE 4**

1. Compute the odd-even reliability of the GGAT.
2. Compute the reliability for a test twice as long as the GGAT.
3. Compute the KR_{20} reliability of the GGAT.
4. Answer the following questions:
   a. Define *reliability* in your own words.

   b. What are some of the major factors contributing to unreliability?

   c. What does the odd-even estimate of reliability tell you about the GGAT? What does KR_{20} tell you?

   d. Explain briefly the rationale of the Spearman-Brown prophecy formula.

LABORATORY EXERCISE 5

Construction of Parallel Forms and Tests of Appropriate Difficulty from the GGAT

PURPOSE

In this exercise, the student will compute the difficulty level and discrimination value (relationship of each item to the total test score) for each item on the GGAT. This information, along with the content of the items, will be used in two ways. First, two parallel forms of the test will be constructed by identifying equivalent items on the basis of content, difficulty, and discrimination values. Second, tests will be constructed that discriminate at different levels of ability.

RELATION TO TOTAL TEST

In Exercise 3, each student administered the GGAT to five people. Considering the total score (number of items answered correctly), the class should identify the examinees who obtained the top 10 scores and the examinees who obtained the bottom 10 scores. For convenience, these extreme scores will be used for further computations in this exercise. The elimination of a portion of the middle scores may influence estimates of difficulty level and item-total correlations. In actual practice, the test constructer would retain all test scores to ensure more stable results.

The relation of the item to the total test score can be computed in a relatively simple manner. The 10 high scores and 10 low scores on the GGAT should be given to two different groups of students. These groups should report the number of the high group and the number of the low group who got each item right. These data should be recorded in Table 5.1. The class will then be able to use Table 5.2 for estimating approximate relationship to total score. Look up the first number (number in the high group) on the left side of the table and the second number (number in the low group) at the top. The correlation is read from the table at the intersection of the appropriate row and column. You will note that the correlation becomes greater (up to 1.00 or -1.00) as the number getting the item correct in the two groups becomes more different. The correlation coefficient used here is the phi coefficient—a statistic appropriate for correlating two variables which are continuous variables that have been reduced artificially to dichotomies.

DIFFICULTY VALUES

An estimate of difficulty is also easy to obtain. Simply add the two numbers (number right in high and low groups), divide by 20, and multiply by 100 to obtain the percent getting the item right. This is only an approximation of the difficulty level, because the middle scorers have not been considered. Note that the difficulty level is a measure of item *ease*—the greater the percent who get the item correct, the higher the difficulty level.

CONSTRUCTION OF PARALLEL FORMS

Parallel forms of a test may be desired for reliability studies or for administrative convenience. In the construction of parallel forms, items should be equated for content, for discrimination value, and for difficulty level. Figure 5.1 provides a schematic method of identifying equivalent items. The item number of each item should be written on the graph at the appropriate place representing the two bits of statistical information for each item. Items nearest each other on the chart should be placed on separate forms. Of course, item content should be taken into account to ensure that the two forms cover the same content in addition to being statistically similar.

Approximately 10 pairs of equivalent items should be selected for the two forms. The original item numbers should be listed in Table 5.3.

In selecting items for the parallel tests, you should select questions with (1) a range of difficulty level, that is, easy, moderately difficult, and hard items; (2) high r values, that is, items which tend to correlate with total test scores; and (3) a wide sample of content in the original GGAT. Items which have a negative r and items which are very easy ($p = 0.95$) or very hard ($p = 0.05$) are probably not very useful on the test.

CONSTRUCTION OF TEST OF APPROPRIATE DIFFICULTY

If the purpose of a test is to discriminate between people at a certain level of ability, the preponderance of items should be of that difficulty level. For example, if the test is to differentiate best from average test takers, the test should consist mainly of hard items. Items should be selected which only a few students pass, that is, items which have a difficulty level around 0.10 to 0.20. Items for this test should be recorded in Table 5.4. The same reasoning applies for selecting items for a test designed to differentiate the poorest examinees from the average group. In this case, easier items (i.e., difficulty level around 0.80 or 0.90) should be selected and listed in Table 5.5.

SUGGESTED READINGS

Anastasi, A. *Psychological Testing* (4th ed.). New York: Macmillan, 1976, pp. 198–226.

Brown, F. G. *Principles of Educational and Psychological Testing* (2nd ed.). New York: Holt, Rinehart and Winston, 1976, pp. 278–283.

Gronlund, N. E. *Measurement and Evaluation in Teaching* (3rd ed.). New York: Macmillan, 1976, pp. 98–99, 110, 113, 120–121, 153–155, 265–267.

Mehrens, W. A., and Lehmann, I. J. *Measurement and Evaluation in Education and Psychology* (2nd ed.). New York: Holt, Rinehart and Winston, 1975, pp. 191–193, 324–329.

Thorndike, R. L., and Hagan, E. *Measurement and Evaluation in Psychology and Education* (4th ed.). New York: Wiley, 1977, pp. 214–216.

Table 5.1 Item Analysis Table

Item	Upper 10 (no. right)	Lower 10 (no. right)	Approximate Relation of Item to Total Score	Approximate Difficulty
1				
2				
3				
4				
5				
6				
7				
8				
9				
10				
11				
12				
13				
14				
15				
16				
17				
18				
19				
20				
21				
22				
23				
24				
25				
26				
27				
28				
29				
30				
31				
32				
33				
34				
35				
36				
37				
38				
39				
40				
41				
42				

Table 5.2 Table for Estimating Approximate Relationship of Item to Total Score

	0	1	2	3	4	5	6	7	8	9	10
10	1.00	.90	.83	.75	.65	.58	.49	.42	.32	.22	.00
9	1.00	.80	.70	.60	.52	.43	.35	.25	.13	.00	−.10
8	1.00	.70	.60	.50	.40	.32	.22	.11	.00	−.13	−.31
7	1.00	.62	.50	.40	.30	.20	.10	.00	−.11	−.25	−.42
6	1.00	.53	.42	.30	.20	.10	.00	−.10	−.22	−.35	−.49
5	1.00	.44	.32	.20	.10	.00	−.10	−.20	−.32	−.43	−.58
4	1.00	.34	.21	.10	.00	−.10	−.20	−.30	−.40	−.52	−.65
3	1.00	.24	.10	.00	−.10	−.20	−.30	−.40	−.50	−.60	−.75
2	1.00	.13	.00	−.10	−.21	−.32	−.42	−.50	−.60	−.70	−.83
1	1.00	.00	−.13	−.24	−.34	−.44	−.53	−.62	−.70	−.80	−.90
0	.00	−1.00	−1.00	−1.00	−1.00	−1.00	−1.00	−1.00	−1.0υ	−1.00	−1.00

Upper 10 (number answering item correctly)

Lower 10 (number answering item correctly)

Note: These correlations are estimates based on the phi coefficient. A reliable item-validity index would require a large number of tests and, depending on the use of the information, might use another index entirely. These approximate scores are used only as an example of the kind of procedure involved in an item analysis.

Approximate Relationship of Item to Total Score

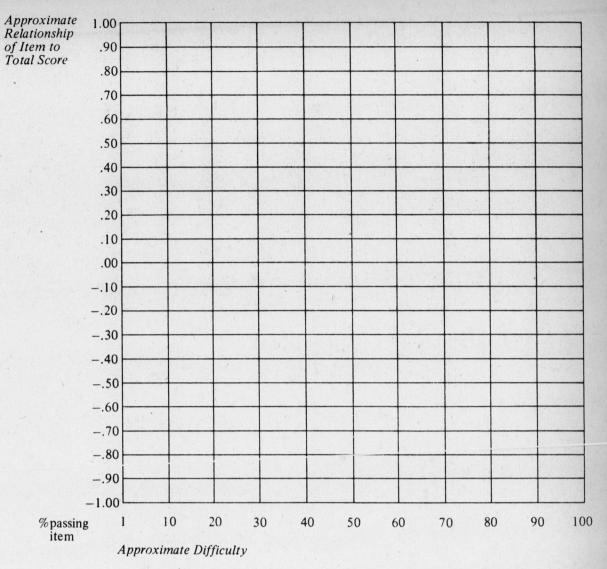

% passing item

Approximate Difficulty

Figure 5.1 Chart for Identifying Equivalent Items

Table 5.3 Parallel Forms
(original GGAT numbers)

	Form A	*Form B*
1.	_____	_____
2.	_____	_____
3.	_____	_____
4.	_____	_____
5.	_____	_____
6.	_____	_____
7.	_____	_____
8.	_____	_____
9.	_____	_____
10.	_____	_____

Table 5.4 "Difficult Test"

1.	_____
2.	_____
3.	_____
4.	_____
5.	_____
6.	_____
7.	_____
8.	_____
9.	_____
10.	_____

Table 5.5 "Easier Test"

1.	_____
2.	_____
3.	_____
4.	_____
5.	_____
6.	_____
7.	_____
8.	_____
9.	_____
10.	_____

Assignment for **EXERCISE 5**

1. Compute item statistics for GGAT (difficulty level and discrimination value).
2. Identify 10 pairs of "equivalent items" considering difficulty level, discrimination value, and item content. List these items in Table 5.3.
3. List items for a test to discriminate the best from the average examinees (Table 5.4) and the poorest from the average examinees (Table 5.5).
4. Answer the following questions:
   a. What are two reasons we might want parallel forms of a test?

   b. In this exercise, you found the discrimination value by correlating items with *total test score*. What other standard or basis of comparison could be used?

   c. How do you think "average" test takers might react to a very difficult test like the one set up in Table 5.4? What can be done to deal with their reactions?

   d. What types of items (in terms of difficulty level and discrimination value) would you select for a test that you wanted to discriminate equally well throughout the entire range of scores?

LABORATORY EXERCISE 6

Building
an Achievement Test:
The Psychological
Achievement Test

PURPOSE

This exercise demonstrates several stages in the development of an achievement test covering basic knowledge from several areas of psychology. The Psychological Achievement Test (PAT) will cover learning, perception, personality, social psychology, physiological psychology, and other areas identified as important by the class. A test plan is prepared to assure content validity, and multiple-choice questions are written. In Exercise 7, item analyses are carried out to evaluate and revise the items.

TEST PLAN

The first step in developing any test is to state the purpose of the test. For this exercise, we might say our purpose is to test college students' knowledge of a wide variety of information about basic psychology. The test might be used to measure how much students know, to evaluate the effectiveness of alternative teaching methods, or to predict success in graduate school. Other validation efforts would be appropriate after these initial test development efforts.

The next step is to prepare a test plan. The construction of achievement tests should follow a plan which assures adequate coverage of the material under consideration. Whether the items are objective (true-false, multiple-choice) or essay, some systematic procedure must be followed so that the sample of items on the test is representative of the population of items which could be included. For the PAT, the test plan will include two dimensions: (1) the *content* of the material and (2) the *cognitive level of understanding* which is measured.

The types of content to be covered might include:

BIOLOGICAL BASES OF BEHAVIOR

Physiological
Comparative
Neuropsychology
Sensation

COGNITIVE-AFFECTIVE BASES OF BEHAVIOR

Learning
Perception
Thinking
Motivation
Emotion

SOCIAL BASES OF BEHAVIOR

Social psychology
Cultural, ethnic, and group processes
Sex roles
Organizational and systems theory

INDIVIDUAL BEHAVIOR

Personality
Human development
Individual differences
Abnormal psychology

The class should add or delete content categories. The test plan can be generated by an examination of introductory textbooks, interviews with instructors, examination of course descriptions, and so on.

The levels of understanding to be covered should include:

Knowledge
Comprehension
Application

These are the lower three "levels" of cognitive understanding taken from Bloom's *Taxonomy of Educational Objectives*. A partial definition of these levels is included in Table 6.1. More complete definitions of these three levels and the top three levels ("Analysis," "Synthesis," "Evaluation") can be obtained from the original source.

Table 6.1 Levels of Cognitive Understanding

1. *Knowledge*—Knowledge is defined as the remembering of previously learned material. This may involve the recall of a wide range of material, from specific facts to complete theories, but all that is required is the bringing to mind of the appropriate information. Knowledge represents the lowest level of learning outcomes in the cognitive domain.

2. *Comprehension*—Comprehension is defined as the ability to grasp the meaning of material. This may be shown by translating material from one form to another (words to numbers), by interpreting material (explaining or summarizing), and by estimating future trends (predicting consequences or effects). These learning outcomes go one step beyond the simple remembering of material, and represent the lowest level of understanding.

3. *Application*—Application refers to the ability to use learned material in new and concrete situations. This may include the application of such things as rules, methods, concepts, principles, laws, and theories. Learning outcomes in this area require a higher level of understanding than those under comprehension.

4. *Analysis*—Analysis refers to the ability to break down material into its component parts so that its organizational structure may be understood. This may include the identification of the parts, analysis of the relationships between parts, and recognition of the organizational principles involved. Learning outcomes here represent a higher intellectual level than comprehension and application because they require an understanding of both the content and the structural form of the material.

5. *Synthesis*—Synthesis refers to the ability to put parts together to form a new whole. This may involve the production of a unique communication (theme or speech), a plan of operations (research proposal), or a set of abstract relations (scheme for clarifying information). Learning outcomes in this area stress creative behaviors, with major emphasis on the formulation of new patterns or structures.

6. *Evaluation*—Evaluation is concerned with the ability to judge the value of material (statement, novel, poem, research report) for a given purpose. The judgments are to be based on definite criteria. These may be internal criteria (organization) or external criteria (relevance to the purpose), and the student may determine the criteria or be given them. Learning outcomes in this area are highest in the cognitive hierarchy because they contain elements of all of the other categories, plus conscious value judgments based on clearly defined criteria.

SOURCE: *Taxonomy of Educational Objectives: Handbook 1: Cognitive Domain*, edited by Benjamin S. Bloom et al. Copyright © 1956 by Longman, Inc. Reprinted by permission of Longman, Inc., New York.

The combination of the content and understanding categories is presented in a two-way table in Table 6.2. The class can alter the categories on the left-hand side of the table. Next, the class should decide what areas of the test should be emphasized. In terms of the content, do you want to have equal numbers of questions on each topic? If so, 25 percent of the items should be in each content area. In terms of objectives, you might want 50 percent of the items to cover knowledge, 25 percent to cover comprehension, and 25 percent for application. The class should come to consensus on the emphasis and write the percentages in the table to guide item writing. Assume you are going to prepare an 80-item test. If 50 percent are to measure knowledge and concurrently 25 percent are to cover biological bases of behavior, then 10 items should be written to measure knowledge of the biological bases of behavior.

ITEM WRITING

Questions should now be written to cover the "cells" of the table. For example, you will write several questions to cover "knowledge of learning," "application of perception," and so on. Number the questions as they are written, and write the item numbers in the table to keep track of coverage. Using the plan ensures giving appropriate coverage and is one step toward content validity. Students might divide the work load, but each student should write a variety of different types of items.

TIPS FOR WRITING QUESTIONS

Once you have decided how many of each type of item to include, the hard part comes: writing the items. In this exercise, you will write multiple-choice items. Some important guidelines to keep in mind when writing multiple-choice items are the following:

1. Each question should contain only one main idea.
2. Item stem and alternatives should be grammatically compatible.
3. Items should be expressed in precise language.
4. Avoid irrelevant sources of difficulty (e.g., difficult vocabulary and jargon).
5. When including negatively worded items, set off the negative aspect by underlining.
6. Avoid the use of words such as *always* and *never*.
7. Offer four or five alternatives.
8. Make the incorrect alternatives plausible.
9. Make the alternatives of equal length.

More detailed directions for writing items are found in the suggested readings.

PREPARING AND ADMINISTERING THE TEST

After the items are written, test forms should be prepared. Space should be provided for name and instructions. The questions should be presented in random order. The instructor will make arrangements to have copies of the test prepared or may ask class members to do so.

Each class member should give the test to five other students. This may be done individually or in a group. The students' answers will be used in Exercise 7 to analyze the difficulty of the items and to determine whether the incorrect alternatives (distractors) are working properly.

SUGGESTED READINGS

Anastasi, A. *Psychological Testing* (4th ed.). New York: Macmillan, 1976, pp. 134–140.

Brown, F. G. *Principles of Educational and Psychological Testing* (2nd ed.). New York: Holt, Rinehart and Winston, 1976, pp. 122–128.

Cronbach, L. J. *Essentials of Psychological Testing* (3rd ed.). New York: Harper & Row, 1970, pp. 145–148, 294–297.

Gronlund, N. E. *Measurement and Evaluation in Teaching* (3rd ed.). New York: Macmillan, 1976, pp. 64–66, 81–84, 135–151, 164–209.

Mehrens, W. A., and Lehmann, I. J. *Measurement and Evaluation in Education and Psychology* (2nd ed.). New York: Holt, Rinehart and Winston, 1975, pp. 110–112, 174–178, 274–290.

Thorndike, R. L., and Hagan, E. *Measurement and Evaluation in Psychology and Education* (4th ed.) New York: Wiley, 1977, pp. 198–245.

Name _____

Directions: Determine the desired distribution of items (percent and number of items) for both content areas and levels of understanding; as you construct items, write the item number in the appropriate space.

Table 6.2 Two-Way Plan for PAT

Content Outline	Knowledge (%) # _____	Comprehension (%) # _____	Application (%) # _____
I. Biological bases of behavior (%) # _____			
II. Cognitive-affective bases of behavior (%) # _____			
III. Social basis of behavior (%) # _____			
IV. Individual behavior (%) # _____			
V. (%) # _____			
VI. (%) # _____			

Levels of Understanding

101

Assignment for **EXERCISE 6**

1. Decide, in the class, what areas should be emphasized, decide how many items of each type should be written, and fill in the numbers on Table 6.2.
2. Examine a variety of sources (books, course descriptions, etc.) and interview experts (instructors, graduate students, etc.) to generate ideas for content categories.
3. Write multiple-choice test items to cover areas in the test plan.
4. Answer the following questions:
   a. Define *content validity*.

   b. For which cells in Table 6.2 was it hardest to write items? Why?

   c. What other factors could be considered in the test plan (in addition to *content* and *levels of understanding*) in the preparation of this test?

LABORATORY EXERCISE 7

Achievement Testing: Item Analysis of the PAT

PURPOSE

For various reasons, the test developer may desire information about the effectiveness of items in a test. We may wish to eliminate some of the items which are too easy or too difficult, to eliminate items which do not differentiate between the better and the poorer students, or, in the case of multiple-choice questions, to revise items which do not have good alternative answers.

This exercise will deal with simple procedures for the evaluation of the effectiveness of individual test items. Three different item-analysis techniques will be carried out. First, item difficulty will be evaluated; second, the discrimination value will be computed; and third, the effectiveness of each alternative will be considered.

DATA COLLECTION

Each class member should administer the PAT to five college-age friends or acquaintances. Score the test by finding the total number of items answered correctly.

From the total pool of subjects tested, extreme groups can be selected for item analysis. The class should select the exam papers with the 10 highest total scores and the 10 lowest total scores. Table 7.1 is used to compile the data. For each chosen paper, record whether the person got each item correct (1) or incorrect (0). The total score is the number of items answered correctly.

DIFFICULTY LEVEL

The difficulty level of an item is defined as the percent of subjects who get an item right. The greater the percent of subjects who get an item right, the higher the difficulty level. In actuality, the difficulty level is a measure of item *ease;* in measurement terminology, the term item *difficulty* is used. There will be no confusion if the student understands the basic definition.

Part I of Table 7.1 is for determining item difficulty. The procedure is similar to that in Exercise 5. The number of subjects in the ''Top 10'' and ''Bottom 10'' who correctly answered each item is recorded at the bottom of the column in the appropriate spaces marked ''Number right.'' The difficulty level is computed by finding the difficulty level in each subgroup, then taking the average of those two numbers.

DISCRIMINATION VALUE

The examiner often wants to know if each item is effectively separating the good and poor examinees. Since the purpose of many achievement tests is to rank individuals with respect to their knowledge of the subject matter, an item can be evaluated on the basis of how well it differentiates between people who do well overall on the test and those who do poorly overall. In general, there are two ways of assessing the discrimination value of items: (1) by computing the difference between the percent of high performing students who get the item right and the percent of low performing students who get the item right, and (2) by correlating the item scores with the scores on the total test.

The difference between percentages of high and low groups can be computed from data in Part I of Table 7.1. Subtract percent low (p_l) from percent high (p_h). If the difference is great, the item is judged to be effective; if there is no difference, the item is not effectively differentiating; if there is a negative difference, the item should probably be discarded or revised because the good students are having more difficulty than the poor students. (*Note*: The larger the difference in percentages, the more effective the item is. There are statistical procedures for evaluating the significance of the difference in proportions. Your instructor may wish to have you calculate such tests. For the purposes of this exercise, you may want to use a rule of thumb that any difference of 20 percent or more is evidence that the item discriminates.)

The correlation of the item and the total test score may be computed in a number of ways. For this exercise, a relatively simple method based on the data already available will be used. The approximate relationship of the item and the total test score may be found in Table 5.2, which provides a quick method of finding a phi coefficient. (The *phi coefficient* is a type of correlation coefficient which should be used when the two variables are both dichotomous.) The table is used by looking up the first number (number in the high group) at the left side of the table and the second number (number in the low group) at the top. The correlation is read from the table at the intersection of the appropriate row and column. The correlation should be recorded in Table 7.1 in the bottom row.

EVALUATION OF ALTERNATIVES

This procedure can be applied to multiple-choice questions. The purpose of the procedure is to study the effectiveness of the incorrect response alternatives (distracters) for each item. The evaluation of alternatives can be carried out in Table 7.2. First, the letter of the correct alternatives should be circled. Next, the percent of the top group answering each alternative and the percent of the bottom group answering each alternative should be recorded. These numbers can be found by collecting the exam papers for the 10 top and 10 bottom papers (based on total scores) and having separate "work groups" compile the data and report to the class. The class as a whole can then find the average percent answering each alternative and record these numbers in the last column.

The student now has information for studying the "performance" of questions and their alternative answers. The difficulty level, discrimination value, and information about alternatives is very helpful in scrutinizing items and revising them.

In the case of an item which is very easy, we may want to revise certain alternatives which are not "attracting" any examinees. It may be that the distracters are illogical or implausible. In the case of an item which has a negative or low discrimination value, we may find that a certain distracter is confusing because it is so close to being correct or because the item deals with a specific instance that only the very knowledgeable examinee understands.

The last column of Table 7.2 gives some indication of the overall "drawing power" of the alternatives. The "distracters" should be plausible yet incorrect. A comparison of the percents in the first two columns indicates if a distracter is doing a proper job of attracting more of the low group than the high group.

REVISION OF ITEMS

Students should now revise a number of questions on the PAT using the item analysis information.

SUGGESTED READINGS

Anastasi, A. *Psychological Testing* (4th ed.). New York: Macmillan, 1976, pp. 198–206, 211–213.

Brown, F. G. *Principles of Educational and Psychological Testing* (2nd ed.). New York: Holt, Rinehart and Winston, 1976, pp. 278–281.

Gronlund, N. E. *Measurement and Evaluation in Teaching* (3rd ed.). New York: Macmillan, 1976, pp. 153–160, 265–271.

Mehrens, W. A., and Lehmann, I. J. *Measurement and Evaluation in Education and Psychology* (2nd ed.). New York: Holt, Rinehart and Winston, 1975, pp. 323–334.

Thorndike, R. L., and Hagan, E. *Measurement and Evaluation in Psychology and Education* (4th ed.). New York: Wiley, 1977, pp. 251–255.

Table 7.1 Computation of Difficulty Level and Discrimination Value for the PAT

	Subject	Item Number																				Total Score for Subject
		1	2	3	4	5	6	7	8	9	10	11	12	13	14	15	16	17	18	19	20	
	1																					
	2																					
	3																					
	4																					
Top 10	5																					
	6																					
	7																					
	8																					
	9																					
	10																					
	11																					
	12																					
	13																					
	14																					
Bottom 10	15																					
	16																					
	17																					
	18																					
	19																					
	20																					

Part I - Difficulty level
  Number right —
  Difficulty level —

Part II - Discrimination value
  Top 10 Number right —
  P_h = % right (top 10) —
  Bottom 10 Number right —
  P_1 = % right (bottom 10) —
  $P_h - P_1$ = —
  Phi coefficient = —

Table 7.2 Evaluating the Performance of Response Alternatives

No.	Alternative	Percent in Top 10 Answering Alternative	Percent in Bottom 10 Answering Alternative	Average Percent Answering Alternative	Item No.	Alternative	Percent in Top 10 Answering Alternative	Percent in Bottom 10 Answering Alternative	Average Percent Answering Alternative
1	1 2 3 4 5				6	1 2 3 4 5			
2	1 2 3 4 5				7	1 2 3 4 5			
3	1 2 3 4 5				8	1 2 3 4 5			
4	1 2 3 4 5				9	1 2 3 4 5			
5	1 2 3 4 5				10	1 2 3 4 5			

Table 7.2 (Continued)

Item No.	Alternative	Percent in Top 10 Answering Alternative	Percent in Bottom 10 Answering Alternative	Average Percent Answering Alternative
11	1			
	2			
	3			
	4			
	5			
12	1			
	2			
	3			
	4			
	5			
13	1			
	2			
	3			
	4			
	5			
14	1			
	2			
	3			
	4			
	5			
15	1			
	2			
	3			
	4			
	5			
16	1			
	2			
	3			
	4			
	5			
17	1			
	2			
	3			
	4			
	5			
18	1			
	2			
	3			
	4			
	5			
19	1			
	2			
	3			
	4			
	5			
20	1			
	2			
	3			
	4			
	5			

Assignment for **EXERCISE 7**

1. Calculate item analysis information in Tables 7.1 and 7.2
2. Revise items specified by your instructor.
3. Answer the following questions.
   a. Define *item analysis*.

   b. List the characteristics of a good "distracter."

   c. What were the main faults with the original questions written by your class for the PAT?

LABORATORY EXERCISE 8

Predictive Validity

PURPOSE

In this exercise, the predictive validity of two tests for selecting applicants to a university will be studied. Test scores for 40 individuals examined in their senior year of high school and their subsequent grade point average (GPA) after the first year of college studies are provided. In this exercise, the student computes correlations between each test and GPA, prepares expectancy tables to show the relationship graphically, and sets up cutting scores to examine different types of prediction errors.

DATA FOR THE EXERCISE

Table 8.1 presents the data. The first column includes test scores for a "College Aptitude Test," a test of verbal comprehension, quantitative reasoning, and abstract thinking. The second test, "World Affairs Test," covers knowledge of current events, political affairs, cultural and sports activities, and general information in recent history. These tests were administered to the students early in their senior year of high school, but the results were not used by university officials in making decisions about whom to select. The test results were "locked up" and not made available to anyone selecting or counseling students, or to any faculty members in the courses.

The reason for not making test scores available to any of the decision makers is to provide a clear examination of the usefulness of the tests over and above the current method of selection. Keeping the test scores from the university faculty reduces the chances that the criterion (GPA) is artificially related to, that is, "contaminated" by, the test scores. In addition, teachers may give additional encouragement to high scorers and ignore low scorers. The research design described here is the only appropriate way to study predictive validity. Unfortunately, practical considerations often lead to the premature use of test scores before they have been properly validated for selection.

The criterion for the research is grade point average (GPA) after one year of studies. This is the cumulative GPA for all courses taken. The students were enrolled in a mixture of majors and courses. A word of caution: GPA at any one point in time may be unreliable and it certainly measures only a limited range of academic performance.

CORRELATIONS

Tables 8.2 and 8.3 should be used to compute the Spearman rank-order correlation between each test and the criterion. (The instructor may ask the class to compute Pearson product-moment correlation coefficients.)

EXPECTANCY TABLE

Next, the student should prepare an expectancy table for the College Aptitude Test. An expectancy table shows the probability of reaching various levels on the criterion (GPA) for each level on the test. For example, if an examinee gets a low score on the test, what is the probability of earning a GPA of 3.5 or above? Tables 8.4 and 8.5 should be used for this step. In Table 8.4, make a tally mark in the "box" corresponding to the test and criterion scores for each subject. On the right-hand side of the table, record the number of subjects at each score level.

In Table 8.5, record the percent of subjects *at each score level* who earn *various grade point averages;* for example, if 10 students get test scores from 501–600, figure out what percent of subjects get a GPA of less than 1.0, 1.0–1.4, and so on. Note that these are "horizontal" percents. Of the total subjects at each score level on the test, what is the probability they will achieve each level of GPA?

The validity coefficient and the expectancy table for any test should be cross-validated on another comparable sample of subjects before it is actually used. Cross-validation should always be done where it is technically feasible. For the purpose of this exercise, cross-validation will not be carried out.

A test which has predictive validity can be used for selection purposes along with other application information. The class should identify what score level could be used to screen future applicants.

DECISION THEORY

The correlation coefficient gives a single, summary index of the predictive validity of the test. The expectancy table shows the probability of getting various GPA's if a student makes a given test score. The scatter plot in Table 8.4 provides additional information about correct and incorrect predictions for individuals. Note that there is a heavy line at the 2.0 GPA. This can be called the *criterion cutoff.* Below this level, students are "on probation," and if they continue to perform this way, they will not graduate. We might say that these students have been "unsuccessful" (at least thus far in their academic careers). Also note that there is a heavy black line at the test score of 500. This can be called the *test cutoff.* Above this line, there is a high probability of success; below the line, a low probability of success. What are these probabilities?

The scatter plot is divided into four segments:

1. High hits—students who scored high on the test and were successful. Correct predictions.
2. False positives—students who scored high on the test but were unsuccessful. Errors in prediction.
3. Low hits—students who scored low on the test and were unsuccessful. Correct predictions.
4. False negatives—students who scored low on the test but were successful. Errors in prediction.

In general, a valid test will result in more correct predictions (hits) than errors.

The interesting, and sometimes tragic, cases are the errors in prediction (segments 2 and 4). If the test were used to make selection decisions about who should be admitted to the university, some individuals would be rejected who would have, in fact, succeeded (false negatives). Some individuals would be accepted who would, in fact, fail (false positives). The realization that a *single* test results in errors of prediction (i.e., false positives and false negatives), leads us to use more than one selection device for assessment. Additional information about applicants can be gathered by interviews, application blanks, letters of recommendation, etc. Even under the best conditions, predictions about academic success are not always accurate. Many unknown and changing factors in the individual and school environment prevent error-free prediction.

SUGGESTED READING

Anastasi, A. *Psychological Testing* (4th ed.). New York: Macmillan, 1976, pp. 140–151.

Brown, F. G. *Principles of Educational and Psychological Testing* (2nd ed.). New York: Holt, Rinehart and Winston, 1976, pp. 97–121.

Cronbach, L. J. *Essentials of Psychological Testing* (3rd ed.). New York: Harper & Row, 1970, pp. 126–142.

Gronlund, N. E. *Measurement and Evaluation in Teaching* (3rd ed.). New York: Macmillan, 1976, pp. 82, 84–93.

Mehrens, W. A., and Lehmann, I. J. *Measurement and Evaluation in Education and Psychology* (2nd ed.). New York: Holt, Rinehart and Winston, 1975, pp. 112–129.

Thorndike, R. L., and Hagan, E. *Measurement and Evaluation in Psychology and Education* (4th ed.). New York: Wiley, 1977, pp. 60–70.

Table 8.1 Test and Criterion Data

Subject	College Aptitude Test	World Affairs Test	GPA
1	618	76	3.9
2	627	36	3.9
3	625	37	3.7
4	681	42	3.6
5	614	47	3.3
6	646	24	3.1
7	396	51	3.0
8	451	57	3.0
9	598	49	2.9
10	595	29	2.9
11	336	55	2.7
12	595	42	2.7
13	785	59	2.6
14	405	41	2.6
15	548	38	2.5
16	600	37	2.5
17	630	75	2.4
18	493	46	2.3
19	590	71	2.2
20	528	62	2.2
21	491	54	2.2
22	540	73	2.0
23	558	67	2.0
24	601	49	2.0
25	481	64	1.7
26	459	62	1.7
27	592	57	1.7
28	505	54	1.7
29	456	45	1.7
30	543	55	1.5
31	438	50	1.5
32	431	53	1.5
33	570	61	1.4
34	206	42	1.4
35	360	39	1.4
36	623	35	1.4
37	512	38	1.3
38	574	38	1.3
39	496	37	0.9
40	381	41	0.5

Table 8.2 Correlation of Aptitude Test and GPA

Subject Number	Rank on Aptitude Test	Rank On GPA	d	d²
1				
2				
3				
4				
5				
6				
7				
8				
9				
10				
11				
12				
13				
14				
15				
16				
17				
18				
19				
20				
21				
22				
23				
24				
25				
26				
27				
28				
29				
30				
31				
32				
33				
34				
35				
36				
37				
38				
39				
40				

$$\Sigma d^2 = \underline{\quad\quad}$$

$$\text{rho} = 1.00 - \left(\frac{6\Sigma d^2}{N^3 - N}\right)$$

Table 8.3 Correlation of World-Affairs Test and GPA

Subject Number	Rank on World Affairs Test	Rank on GPA	d	d²
1				
2				
3				
4				
5				
6				
7				
8				
9				
10				
11				
12				
13				
14				
15				
16				
17				
18				
19				
20				
21				
22				
23				
24				
25				
26				
27				
28				
29				
30				
31				
32				
33				
34				
35				
36				
37				
38				
39				
40				

$$\Sigma d^2 = \underline{\quad}$$

$$\text{rho} = 1.00 \left(\frac{6 \Sigma d^2}{N^3 - N} \right)$$

Table 8.4 Scatter Plot of Test and Criterion Data

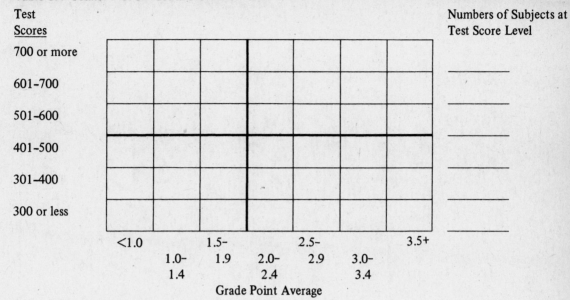

Table 8.5 Expectancy Table

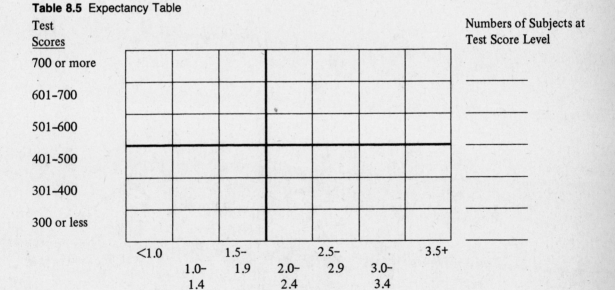

Assignment for **EXERCISE 8**

1. Compute correlations of the tests and the criterion.
2. Prepare the scatter plot and expectancy table for the college aptitude test.
3. It should be emphasized that the validity estimates, expectancy tables, and decision rules should be cross-validated whenever possible. For the purpose of this exercise, assume cross-validation was successful. Now, answer the following questions:
   a. What would you advise the following two students?

	College aptitude score	*World affairs score*
Sally:	275	50
Bob:	625	58

   Bob:

   Sally:

   b. What might explain false positives, that is, the cases in which high-scoring students fail in school?

   c. What could be done in a practical way to deal with false positives and with potential false negatives?

LABORATORY EXERCISE 9

Selection, Differential Validity, and Discrimination

PURPOSE

This exercise is designed to give the student an opportunity to work with problems of differential validity and discrimination. Although these two concepts are related, they are different. They are important concepts related to testing and fair employment practices, and to college admissions.

BACKGROUND

Legislation, policies, and testing guidelines issued by the United States government in recent years give organizations the responsibility of demonstrating that their selection tests are valid and that they do not discriminate unfairly against members of groups covered by the law. Validity can be demonstrated in a number of ways: content validity, criterion validity including concurrent and predictive methods, and construct validity. In each case, the organization must present documented evidence that the test measures the knowledge, skills, and abilities required for successful completion of job duties.

In this exercise, predictive validity is illustrated. *Predictive validity* is a statistically demonstrated relationship (usually a correlation coefficient) between the selection test and "on-the-job" performance. Tests should not be used if performance on the test has no relationship to job performance. To be valid, a test must be shown to correlate significantly with a criterion of job performance.

A selection test, however, may achieve validity for the entire set of persons but may not achieve validity for a particular subset of those persons. *Differential validity* exists when subsets (e.g., males versus females, majority versus minority) have different validity coefficients. Differential validity can lead to discrimination. A test is said to discriminate unfairly against a subset of people if members of the group obtain lower scores on the test than other applicants but do not perform at a lower level on the job.

CASE STUDY

The Acme Company has done a predictive-validation study of a manual dexterity test that it wishes to use for selecting assemblers in its electrical products factory. Although the validity coefficient was significant, it was not very high. Since their validation sample of 60 employees was composed of 30 men and 30 women, the personnel department thought that their test might be more valid for one group than for another. Also, in order to comply with testing guidelines, they decided to check whether their test was discriminating against either the men or women.

Table 9.1 shows the test scores and performance ratings for men and women. Based on past experience, the company considers a criterion rating of 30 or above to indicate successful performance on the job.

PROCEDURE

Follow the directions in the assignment for this exercise. (In this exercise, the student is asked to compute the Pearson product-moment correlation coefficient. The Pearson r is the most commonly used procedure for calculating a correlation and thus is included here to give the student exposure to it. The instructor may wish to have students calculate the Spearman rank-difference correlation for convenience.)

SUGGESTED READINGS

Anastasi, A. *Psychological Testing* (4th ed.). New York: Macmillan, 1976, pp. 90–197.

Brown, F. G. *Principles of Educational and Psychological Testing* (2nd ed.). New York: Holt, Rinehart and Winston, 1976, pp. 109–110.

Cronbach, L. J. *Essentials of Psychological Testing* (3rd ed.). New York: Harper & Row, 1970, pp. 406–451.

Gronlund, N. E. *Measurement and Evaluation in Teaching* (3rd ed.). New York: Macmillan, 1976, pp. 553–556.

Mehrens, W. A., and Lehmann, I. J. *Measurement and Evaluation in Education and Psychology* (2nd ed.). New York: Holt, Rinehart and Winston, 1975, pp. 674–681.

Thorndike, R. L., and Hagan, E. *Measurement and Evaluation in Psychology and Education* (4th ed.). New York: Wiley, 1977, pp. 617–618.

Table 9.1 Test and Criterion Scores for 60 Employees

Men (m)			Women (w)		
Employee #	X	Y	Employee #	X	Y
1	23	4	2	33	27
3	37	13	4	35	22
5	34	21	6	34	36
7	36	28	8	40	34
9	32	35	10	49	14
11	42	13	11	45	17
13	46	16	14	43	22
15	42	25	16	44	28
17	44	23	18	41	26
19	47	28	20	44	29
21	49	27	22	49	34
23	46	33	24	47	35
25	43	35	26	48	38
27	41	38	28	44	46
29	45	47	30	46	41
31	54	16	32	54	13
33	56	22	34	56	16
35	55	23	36	53	24
37	53	27	38	59	29
39	59	39	40	54	25
41	56	37	42	53	34
43	58	32	44	56	32
45	51	34	46	53	37
47	55	49	48	59	34
49	55	43	50	58	42
51	67	25	52	51	46
53	63	36	54	64	27
55	64	37	56	66	26
57	61	44	58	68	32
59	75	51	60	75	33

Note: X = test score; Y = sum of supervisor ratings.

Assignment and Procedure for **EXERCISE 9**

SELECTION AND TEST-DISCRIMINATION EXERCISE

1. Draw separate scatter plots for men and women on the graphs provided in Figure 9.1. Compare the scatter plots. Do they appear similar? What might this lead you to believe?

2. Calculate separate correlation coefficients (r) for men and women. Use the formulas below:

(for men) $$r_m = \frac{N\Sigma X_m Y_m - \Sigma X_m Y_m}{\sqrt{\left[N\Sigma X_m^2 - (\Sigma X_m)^2\right]\left[N\Sigma Y_m^2 - (\Sigma Y_m)^2\right]}}$$

(for women) $$r_w = \frac{N\Sigma X_w Y_w - \Sigma X_w Y_w}{\sqrt{\left[N\Sigma X_w^2 - (\Sigma X_w)^2\right]\left[N\Sigma Y_w^2 - (\Sigma Y_w)^2\right]}}$$

N = number of employees (men or women) = 30
X = test score
Y = performance ratings

r_m = _____ r_w = _____

Refer to the following significance levels in interpreting the coefficients: with $N = 30$, a correlation of .361 is significant at p .05, and a correlation of .463 is significant at p .01. (These values were obtained from a table of significant r values contained in numerous statistics books.) What do these coefficients indicate concerning the validity of the test score for men? for women?

3. Next, consider whether the validities are different from each other. The procedures for testing the statistical significance of the differences in two correlation coefficients is complicated and will not be presented here. Does it appear that the r's are actually different from each other?_____Under what conditions could a test be *valid* for Group A and *not valid* for Group B, yet demonstrate *no differential validity?*

4. Calculate the mean test scores and mean performance scores for men and women.
   a. Do the test means seem to be any different for men and women?
   b. Do the supervisory ratings seem to be different for the two groups?

5. Complete the next tables by computing the probability of success for men and women employees in each test-score category. The probability of success is computed by dividing the number of successful employees in each category by the total number in the category. ("Success" requires 30 or above on the criterion.)

Test Scores	No. employees	No. successful	Probability of success
Men			
71 or above			
61 or above			
51 or above			
40 or above			
31 or above			
21 or above			
Women			
71 or above			
61 or above			
51 or above			
41 or above			
31 or above			
21 or above			

6. Suppose the Acme Company had decided to hire only those applicants receiving 61 or above on the test.
   a. How many men would they have hired?_____
   b. How many women would they have hired?_____
   c. What would have been the probability of success for men hired?_____
   d. What would have been the probability of success for women hired?_____
   e. Would there be any unfair discrimination? Against whom?_____

7. Suppose the Acme Company had decided to hire only those applicants receiving 21 or above on the test.
   a. How many men would they have hired?_____
   b. How many women would they have hired?_____
   c. What would have been the probability of success for men hired?_____
   d. What would have been the probability of success for women hired?_____
   e. Would there be any unfair discrimination of either group?_____

8. Would it be appropriate to use the test for hiring both men and women? It should be emphasized that cross-validation (see Exercise 11) be carried out whenever possible before a test is used in practice. For the purpose of this exercise, assume cross-validation was successful.

9. What would you suggest to the personnel department of the Acme Company as a way of improving the accuracy of its selection procedures? (Remember that federal regulations prohibit hiring practices which are unfair to a particular group.)

Figure 9.1 Scatter Plots Showing Relationships of Test Scores and Criterion
Measures for Men and Women

Men

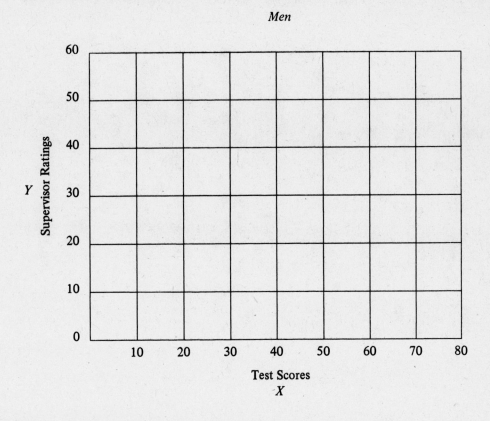

Women

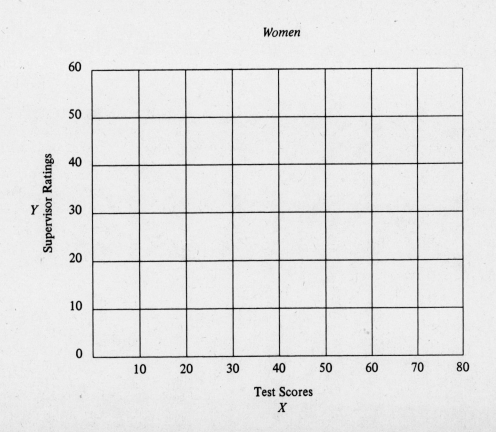

LABORATORY EXERCISE 10

Empirical Construction of Scales for the Personal Orientation Test

PURPOSE

This exercise is designed to demonstrate the technique of empirical scale construction. Scales will be built to measure five separate categories of leisure-time interests of college students: gaming, sporting, gourmet, aesthetic, and social orientations. The items on the Personal Orientation Test (POT) were written to reflect activities, preferences, and behaviors associated with the five categories.

The method of empirical scale construction, often called criterion keying, will allow the class to identify items which actually differentiate the interests of people known to have gaming, social, gourmet, aesthetic, and social interests from the interests of a students-in-general group.

Each student in class will administer the POT to friends or acquaintances who manifest the interests and frequently engage in the behaviors defined for each of the five leisure-time orientations. The responses of each of these criterion groups will be compared separately to the responses of a students-in-general group. Items which actually differentiate the activities, interests, and preferences of each criterion group from the students-in-general group will be selected for the five scales.

Norm tables will be established for each scale and test profiles prepared. Cross-validation will be carried out in Exercise 11.

PROCEDURE

1. *Identification of criterion groups.* Obviously, the selection of the criterion groups is a critical step in this process. The scale that is to be constructed will, because of the nature of the process, differentiate between the criterion group and the students-in-general group; however, if the criterion group is badly picked, the scale may not identify the characteristic being evaluated. In this exercise, the student must use good judgment to identify members of the criterion groups.

   The definition of each criterion group is listed in Table 10.1. The class should discuss the characteristics of the different groups until they have as clear a picture as possible of the individuals they will ask to participate.

2. *Administration of the test to the criterion groups.* Each student should locate two persons for each criterion group and test both of them. In asking the subject to volunteer, care should be taken so that the response pattern the subject is expected to have is not suggested ahead of time.

3. *Administration of the test to the students-in-general group.* General student groups are needed for three steps in the process: (1) for test development, that is, the selection of items for scales; (2) for preparing norm tables; and (3) for cross-validation in Exercise 11. Therefore, three students who do not manifest high interests in any criterion area are needed for each class member.

   Norm group subjects may be obtained in several ways. The instructor may ask class members to complete the POT before the exercise and criterion categories are discussed. Class members may give the POT to three friends and acquaintances who do not fit into any of the criterion groups. Or, an introductory class or another class can be used to provide a readily available, if nonrandom, subject group. In this case, the instructor will collect three copies of the POT from each student and arrange testing of this group.

After the students-in-general group subjects are tested, their papers should be randomly divided into three groups and used for the three purposes stated at the beginning of this step.

4. *Tabulation of responses to the individual items.* Each student should select randomly one of the two tests administered to the members of the "gaming" criterion group. (One test will be used for development of the scales; the other will be used for cross-validation in Exercise 11.) All the tests so selected for the "gaming" group should be gathered together and given to a work group of four to six students. This work group can tabulate the number of "true" responses to each of the 45 items and report back to the class the percent of subjects in the "gaming" group who responded "true" to each item. Simultaneously, other work groups can be tabulating the responses for the tests of the other criterion groups and one-third of the general student group. These data should be recorded in Table 10.2

5. *Selection of items that differentiate.* Items are now identified which belong on the various scales. The percent responding "true" in the students-in-general group is subtracted from the percent responding "true" in the "gaming" group and entered into the column headed $\triangle$. The "plus" or "minus" sign should be recorded because this shows the direction of the difference. These differences show which items differentiate between the criterion and general group and the direction of that difference. A "plus" difference means that a "true" response is more like the gaming individuals. In actual test construction, statistics would be calculated indicating the probability that a difference this large or larger could have occurred by chance. For the purposes of this exercise, the student should simply pick those items that show the largest differences, arbitrarily selecting between 12 and 15 items for each scale. The scoring key for each scale should be listed in Table 10.3. For each scale ("Gaming," "Sporting," etc.), this will show the items on that scale, and the "keyed" answer indicates whether "true" or "false" is the answer most like the responses of criterion group. There may be items which differentiate in the same way for more than one group. It is permissible to place one item on two scales; for example, the same item may indicate both Gaming and Social orientation. It would be undesirable if two scales had more than three or four items in common. If a large number of items (say over 50 percent) are on two scales, they are not measuring separate constructs, and the result will be a high correlation between the scales.

6. *Establishment of norms for the scales.* After the items on each scale are identified, the tests of a norm group should be scored. (The norm group for this exercise will be one-third of the students-in-general group.) The score on each scale is the number of discriminating items that the person answered in the same way as did the criterion group. A large number of "right" (i.e., keyed) answers results in a high score and indicates many responses like those of that criterion group. Each norm-group test will have five scores, one score on each of the five scales. The work groups can be given a number of the norm-group tests to score. Percentile norms should be computed for the distribution of scores on each of the five scales in Tables 10.4 to 10.8.

7. *Cross-validation of the scale on a new criterion group.* The cross-validation procedure is carried out in Exercise 11.

8. Profile of individual tests. The test is now ready to use. It can now be scored on the five scales, and test profiles can be prepared. The student can give the test to someone and can then "interpret" the profile in the light of other general information about the individual and other test data which may have been obtained from this workbook. (In the actual use of tests, it is essential that the test has been cross-validated. For purposes of this exercise, the instructor may not insist on cross-validation before carrying out this step.) Profiles can be prepared for your criterion and norm group subjects, although this would normally not be done.

SUGGESTED READINGS

Anastasi, A. *Psychological Testing* (4th ed.). New York: Macmillan, 1976, pp. 496–506, 529, 538–539.

Brown, F. G. *Principles of Educational and Psychological Testing* (2nd ed.). New York: Holt, Rinehart and Winston, 1976, pp. 362–382.

Cronbach, L. J. *Essentials of Psychological Testing* (3rd ed.). New York: Harper & Row, 1970, pp. 460–463.

Mehrens, W. A., and Lehmann, I. J. *Measurement and Evaluation in Education and Psychology* (2nd ed.). New York: Holt, Rinehart and Winston, 1975, pp. 550–558.

Table 10.1 Description of Criterion Characteristics for Construction of Scales on the Personal Orientation Test

Gaming: This person spends a great deal of time playing games of one form or another. He or she may play chess, bridge, checkers, or other games. The person may be addicted to one particular game or may play many different games. If given a choice of how to spend free time, he or she would most frequently prefer playing a game of some kind.

Sporting: This person has a strong interest in athletics and is personally involved in many athletic activities. He or she is not simply a member of an athletic team, but spends a considerable amount of time keeping in condition and enjoys athletic activities. If given a choice as to how to spend free time, he or she would most frequently prefer some kind of active participation in a competitive sport.

Gourmet: This person is characterized by a high interest in fine foods and beverages. He or she enjoys dining in fine restaurants and possesses appetites for rare and unusual foods. The person would probably enjoy foreign foods, fine cheeses, and would prefer to spend free time dining out or preparing unusual dishes alone or for friends. (Note: Weight is not important; it is the general orientation toward good food that is critical.)

Aesthetic: This person has a strong preference for the fine arts, including music, painting, sculpture, dramatics, and/or the dance. He or she may be interested and involved in many different activities or caught up completely in one. Free time is spent involved in creative activities or going to plays, concerts, or museums.

Social: This person enjoys social gatherings, parties, bull sessions, and generally being with other people. He or she is rarely alone, has a wide circle of acquaintances, and if one friend is busy, typically seeks other friends to spend time with. Free time is spent with other people, *never* alone.

Table 10.2 Tabulation Sheet for Scale Construction on Personal Orientation Test

	Gaming "True" Responses			Sporting "True" Responses			Gourmet "True" Responses			Aesthetic "True" Responses			Social "True" Responses			Students-in-General "True" Responses	
Item	No.	%	Δ	No.	%	Δ	No.	%	Δ	No.	%	Δ	No.	%	Δ	No.	%
1																	
2																	
3																	
4																	
5																	
6																	
7																	
8																	
9																	
10																	
11																	
12																	
13																	
14																	
15																	
16																	
17																	
18																	
19																	
20																	
21																	
22																	

Table 10.2 (Continued)

Item	Gaming "True" Responses No.	Gaming "True" Responses %	Gaming "True" Responses Δ	Sporting "True" Responses No.	Sporting "True" Responses %	Sporting "True" Responses Δ	Gourmet "True" Responses No.	Gourmet "True" Responses %	Gourmet "True" Responses Δ	Aesthetic "True" Responses No.	Aesthetic "True" Responses %	Aesthetic "True" Responses Δ	Social "True" Responses No.	Social "True" Responses %	Social "True" Responses Δ	Students-in-General "True" Responses No.	Students-in-General "True" Responses %
23																	
24																	
25																	
26																	
27																	
28																	
29																	
30																	
31																	
32																	
33																	
34																	
35																	
36																	
37																	
38																	
39																	
40																	
41																	
42																	
43																	
44																	
45																	

Table 10.3 Scoring Keys for Scales of POT

	Gaming Key			Sporting Key			Gourmet Key	
	Original Item Number	*"Keyed" Answer*		*Original Item Number*	*"Keyed" Answer*		*Original Item Number*	*"Keyed" Answer*
1			1			1		
2			2			2		
3			3			3		
4			4			4		
5			5			5		
6			6			6		
7			7			7		
8			8			8		
9			9			9		
10			10			10		
11			11			11		
12			12			12		
13			13			13		
14			14			14		
15			15			15		

	Aesthetic Key			Social Key	
	Original Item Number	*"Keyed" Answer*		*Original Item Number*	*"Keyed" Answer*
1			1		
2			2		
3			3		
4			4		
5			5		
6			6		
7			7		
8			8		
9			9		
10			10		
11			11		
12			12		
13			13		
14			14		
15			15		

Table 10.4 Gaming

	Tabulation	Average Rank	%ile
15			
14			
13			
12			
11			
10			
9			
8			
7			
6			
5			
4			
3			
2			
1			

Table 10.5 Sporting

	Tabulation	Average Rank	%ile
15			
14			
13			
12			
11			
10			
9			
8			
7			
6			
5			
4			
3			
2			
1			

Table 10.6 Gourmet

	Tabulation	Average Rank	%ile
15			
14			
13			
12			
11			
10			
9			
8			
7			
6			
5			
4			
3			
2			
1			

Table 10.7 Aesthetic

	Tabulation	Average Rank	%ile
15			
14			
13			
12			
11			
10			
9			
8			
7			
6			
5			
4			
3			
2			
1			

Table 10.8 Social

	Tabulation	Average Rank	%ile
15			
14			
13			
12			
11			
10			
9			
8			
7			
6			
5			
4			
3			
2			
1			

Assignment for **EXERCISE 10**

1. Administer the POT to two individuals who, in your judgment, fit each of the five criterion groups. (*Optional*: Test three students with general interests.)
2. After the scoring keys and norms have been prepared, give the test to an acquaintance, score it, prepare a test profile, and write an interpretation of the profile.
3. Discuss the test results with the person you tested. (*Note*: The instructor may wish to delay assignments two and three until after cross-validation.)
4. Answer the following questions:
   a. What technical inadequacies do you see in items on the POT?

   b. Examine the content of the items on each scale. Do they "make sense" in relation to the criterion categories?

   c. What are the advantages of the empirical test-construction procedure?

   d. What difficulties, if any, did you encounter when discussing results with the examinee? What did you learn from the experience?

Examinee _____

Examiner _____

Personal Orientation Test

Answer the following items true or false. Answer every item. It is your opinion that is important. There are no right or wrong answers.

T   F

☐ ☐   1. I like art museums.

☐ ☐   2. I like to exercise just for the fun of it.

☐ ☐   3. Life is a challenge.

☐ ☐   4. I have several items of sport's equipment in my room.

☐ ☐   5. I buy a new book or magazine every week.

☐ ☐   6. I prefer having a roommate to living alone.

☐ ☐   7. I prefer exotic foreign foods to ordinary meals.

☐ ☐   8. I would rather listen to music than play cards.

☐ ☐   9. Participation in sports develops initiative.

☐ ☐   10. Chess teaches logical thinking and concentration.

☐ ☐   11. I would rather dine in a good restaurant than go to an informal party.

☐ ☐   12. Monopoly is more fun than bridge.

☐ ☐   13. I like intellectual challenges.

☐ ☐   14. I like the out-of-doors.

☐ ☐   15. I would rather read than watch TV.

☐ ☐   16. I prefer studying in the student center to studying in my room.

☐ ☐   17. I would rather work in a job I enjoy than travel.

☐ ☐   18. After studying for a while I have to go talk to someone before I can concentrate again.

☐ ☐   19. I smoke heavily.

☐ ☐   20. I prefer a ball game to a concert.

☐ ☐   21. I think Picasso's art is phony.

☐ ☐   22. I prefer light music to heavy symphonies.

☐ ☐   23. Card games are a waste of time.

T	F	
□	□	24. I would rather have wine than milk with a meal.
□	□	25. I know more about foods than most people.
□	□	26. Feeling physically fit is important to me.
□	□	27. Puzzles tend to sharpen your mind.
□	□	28. To do good work in school, it is necessary to be in good physical condition.
□	□	29. I would rather sit in on a bull session than read.
□	□	30. People who play a lot of bridge tend to do poorly in school.
□	□	31. The scent of food is disagreeable to many people.
□	□	32. I would rather grab a quick snack than sit over a long meal in the evening.
□	□	33. The person who enjoys ballet is usually not very well adjusted socially.
□	□	34. Modern art is a reflection of confused minds.
□	□	35. I eat a lot of different kinds of cheeses.
□	□	36. I would rather have steak and potatoes than some kind of foreign food.
□	□	37. I play classical music all the time I am in my room.
□	□	38. I attend almost all the plays that are presented.
□	□	39. I prefer reading to attending a football game.
□	□	40. I have a personal library of over 50 books in my room, not counting textbooks.
□	□	41. I have many friends.
□	□	42. I don't like to eat alone.
□	□	43. I like hunting and fishing.
□	□	44. I would rather play cards or chess than simply sit and read.
□	□	45. I have only one or two close friends.

Examinee _____ 147
Examiner _____

Personal Orientation Test

Answer the following items true or false. Answer every item. It is your opinion that is important. There are no right or wrong answers.

T F

☐ ☐ 1. I like art museums.

☐ ☐ 2. I like to exercise just for the fun of it.

☐ ☐ 3. Life is a challenge.

☐ ☐ 4. I have several items of sport's equipment in my room.

☐ ☐ 5. I buy a new book or magazine every week.

☐ ☐ 6. I prefer having a roommate to living alone.

☐ ☐ 7. I prefer exotic foreign foods to ordinary meals.

☐ ☐ 8. I would rather listen to music than play cards.

☐ ☐ 9. Participation in sports develops initiative.

☐ ☐ 10. Chess teaches logical thinking and concentration.

☐ ☐ 11. I would rather dine in a good restaurant than go to an informal party.

☐ ☐ 12. Monopoly is more fun than bridge.

☐ ☐ 13. I like intellectual challenges.

☐ ☐ 14. I like the out-of-doors.

☐ ☐ 15. I would rather read than watch TV.

☐ ☐ 16. I prefer studying in the student center to studying in my room.

☐ ☐ 17. I would rather work in a job I enjoy than travel.

☐ ☐ 18. After studying for a while I have to go talk to someone before I can concentrate again.

☐ ☐ 19. I smoke heavily.

☐ ☐ 20. I prefer a ball game to a concert.

☐ ☐ 21. I think Picasso's art is phony.

☐ ☐ 22. I prefer light music to heavy symphonies.

☐ ☐ 23. Card games are a waste of time.

☐ ☐   24. I would rather have wine than milk with a meal.

☐ ☐   25. I know more about foods than most people.

☐ ☐   26. Feeling physically fit is important to me.

☐ ☐   27. Puzzles tend to sharpen your mind.

☐ ☐   28. To do good work in school, it is necessary to be in good physical condition.

☐ ☐   29. I would rather sit in on a bull session than read.

☐ ☐   30. People who play a lot of bridge tend to do poorly in school.

☐ ☐   31. The scent of food is disagreeable to many people.

☐ ☐   32. I would rather grab a quick snack than sit over a long meal in the evening.

☐ ☐   33. The person who enjoys ballet is usually not very well adjusted socially.

☐ ☐   34. Modern art is a reflection of confused minds.

☐ ☐   35. I eat a lot of different kinds of cheeses.

☐ ☐   36. I would rather have steak and potatoes than some kind of foreign food.

☐ ☐   37. I play classical music all the time I am in my room.

☐ ☐   38. I attend almost all the plays that are presented.

☐ ☐   39. I prefer reading to attending a football game.

☐ ☐   40. I have a personal library of over 50 books in my room, not counting textbooks.

☐ ☐   41. I have many friends.

☐ ☐   42. I don't like to eat alone.

☐ ☐   43. I like hunting and fishing.

☐ ☐   44. I would rather play cards or chess than simply sit and read.

☐ ☐   45. I have only one or two close friends.

Personal Orientation Test

Answer the following items true or false. Answer every item. It is your opinion that is important. There are no right or wrong answers.

T   F

☐ ☐   1. I like art museums.

☐ ☐   2. I like to exercise just for the fun of it.

☐ ☐   3. Life is a challenge.

☐ ☐   4. I have several items of sport's equipment in my room.

☐ ☐   5. I buy a new book or magazine every week.

☐ ☐   6. I prefer having a roommate to living alone.

☐ ☐   7. I prefer exotic foreign foods to ordinary meals.

☐ ☐   8. I would rather listen to music than play cards.

☐ ☐   9. Participation in sports develops initiative.

☐ ☐   10. Chess teaches logical thinking and concentration.

☐ ☐   11. I would rather dine in a good restaurant than go to an informal party.

☐ ☐   12. Monopoly is more fun than bridge.

☐ ☐   13. I like intellectual challenges.

☐ ☐   14. I like the out-of-doors.

☐ ☐   15. I would rather read than watch TV.

☐ ☐   16. I prefer studying in the student center to studying in my room.

☐ ☐   17. I would rather work in a job I enjoy than travel.

☐ ☐   18. After studying for a while I have to go talk to someone before I can concentrate again.

☐ ☐   19. I smoke heavily.

☐ ☐   20. I prefer a ball game to a concert.

☐ ☐   21. I think Picasso's art is phony.

☐ ☐   22. I prefer light music to heavy symphonies.

☐ ☐   23. Card games are a waste of time.

T   F

☐ ☐   24. I would rather have wine than milk with a meal.

☐ ☐   25. I know more about foods than most people.

☐ ☐   26. Feeling physically fit is important to me.

☐ ☐   27. Puzzles tend to sharpen your mind.

☐ ☐   28. To do good work in school, it is necessary to be in good physical condition.

☐ ☐   29. I would rather sit in on a bull session than read.

☐ ☐   30. People who play a lot of bridge tend to do poorly in school.

☐ ☐   31. The scent of food is disagreeable to many people.

☐ ☐   32. I would rather grab a quick snack than sit over a long meal in the evening.

☐ ☐   33. The person who enjoys ballet is usually not very well adjusted socially.

☐ ☐   34. Modern art is a reflection of confused minds.

☐ ☐   35. I eat a lot of different kinds of cheeses.

☐ ☐   36. I would rather have steak and potatoes than some kind of foreign food.

☐ ☐   37. I play classical music all the time I am in my room.

☐ ☐   38. I attend almost all the plays that are presented.

☐ ☐   39. I prefer reading to attending a football game.

☐ ☐   40. I have a personal library of over 50 books in my room, not counting textbooks.

☐ ☐   41. I have many friends.

☐ ☐   42. I don't like to eat alone.

☐ ☐   43. I like hunting and fishing.

☐ ☐   44. I would rather play cards or chess than simply sit and read.

☐ ☐   45. I have only one or two close friends.

Personal Orientation Test

Answer the following items true or false. Answer every item. It is your opinion that is important. There are no right or wrong answers.

T   F

☐ ☐   1. I like art museums.

☐ ☐   2. I like to exercise just for the fun of it.

☐ ☐   3. Life is a challenge.

☐ ☐   4. I have several items of sport's equipment in my room.

☐ ☐   5. I buy a new book or magazine every week.

☐ ☐   6. I prefer having a roommate to living alone.

☐ ☐   7. I prefer exotic foreign foods to ordinary meals.

☐ ☐   8. I would rather listen to music than play cards.

☐ ☐   9. Participation in sports develops initiative.

☐ ☐   10. Chess teaches logical thinking and concentration.

☐ ☐   11. I would rather dine in a good restaurant than go to an informal party.

☐ ☐   12. Monopoly is more fun than bridge.

☐ ☐   13. I like intellectual challenges.

☐ ☐   14. I like the out-of-doors.

☐ ☐   15. I would rather read than watch TV.

☐ ☐   16. I prefer studying in the student center to studying in my room.

☐ ☐   17. I would rather work in a job I enjoy than travel.

☐ ☐   18. After studying for a while I have to go talk to someone before I can concentrate again.

☐ ☐   19. I smoke heavily.

☐ ☐   20. I prefer a ball game to a concert.

☐ ☐   21. I think Picasso's art is phony.

☐ ☐   22. I prefer light music to heavy symphonies.

☐ ☐   23. Card games are a waste of time.

153

T   F

☐ ☐   24. I would rather have wine than milk with a meal.

☐ ☐   25. I know more about foods than most people.

☐ ☐   26. Feeling physically fit is important to me.

☐ ☐   27. Puzzles tend to sharpen your mind.

☐ ☐   28. To do good work in school, it is necessary to be in good physical condition.

☐ ☐   29. I would rather sit in on a bull session than read.

☐ ☐   30. People who play a lot of bridge tend to do poorly in school.

☐ ☐   31. The scent of food is disagreeable to many people.

☐ ☐   32. I would rather grab a quick snack than sit over a long meal in the evening.

☐ ☐   33. The person who enjoys ballet is usually not very well adjusted socially.

☐ ☐   34. Modern art is a reflection of confused minds.

☐ ☐   35. I eat a lot of different kinds of cheeses.

☐ ☐   36. I would rather have steak and potatoes than some kind of foreign food.

☐ ☐   37. I play classical music all the time I am in my room.

☐ ☐   38. I attend almost all the plays that are presented.

☐ ☐   39. I prefer reading to attending a football game.

☐ ☐   40. I have a personal library of over 50 books in my room, not counting textbooks.

☐ ☐   41. I have many friends.

☐ ☐   42. I don't like to eat alone.

☐ ☐   43. I like hunting and fishing.

☐ ☐   44. I would rather play cards or chess than simply sit and read.

☐ ☐   45. I have only one or two close friends.

Personal Orientation Test

Answer the following items true or false. Answer every item. It is your opinion that is important. There are no right or wrong answers.

T   F

☐ ☐   1. I like art museums.

☐ ☐   2. I like to exercise just for the fun of it.

☐ ☐   3. Life is a challenge.

☐ ☐   4. I have several items of sport's equipment in my room.

☐ ☐   5. I buy a new book or magazine every week.

☐ ☐   6. I prefer having a roommate to living alone.

☐ ☐   7. I prefer exotic foreign foods to ordinary meals.

☐ ☐   8. I would rather listen to music than play cards.

☐ ☐   9. Participation in sports develops initiative.

☐ ☐   10. Chess teaches logical thinking and concentration.

☐ ☐   11. I would rather dine in a good restaurant than go to an informal party.

☐ ☐   12. Monopoly is more fun than bridge.

☐ ☐   13. I like intellectual challenges.

☐ ☐   14. I like the out-of-doors.

☐ ☐   15. I would rather read than watch TV.

☐ ☐   16. I prefer studying in the student center to studying in my room.

☐ ☐   17. I would rather work in a job I enjoy than travel.

☐ ☐   18. After studying for a while I have to go talk to someone before I can concentrate again.

☐ ☐   19. I smoke heavily.

☐ ☐   20. I prefer a ball game to a concert.

☐ ☐   21. I think Picasso's art is phony.

☐ ☐   22. I prefer light music to heavy symphonies.

☐ ☐   23. Card games are a waste of time.

T	F	
☐	☐	24. I would rather have wine than milk with a meal.
☐	☐	25. I know more about foods than most people.
☐	☐	26. Feeling physically fit is important to me.
☐	☐	27. Puzzles tend to sharpen your mind.
☐	☐	28. To do good work in school, it is necessary to be in good physical condition.
☐	☐	29. I would rather sit in on a bull session than read.
☐	☐	30. People who play a lot of bridge tend to do poorly in school.
☐	☐	31. The scent of food is disagreeable to many people.
☐	☐	32. I would rather grab a quick snack than sit over a long meal in the evening.
☐	☐	33. The person who enjoys ballet is usually not very well adjusted socially.
☐	☐	34. Modern art is a reflection of confused minds.
☐	☐	35. I eat a lot of different kinds of cheeses.
☐	☐	36. I would rather have steak and potatoes than some kind of foreign food.
☐	☐	37. I play classical music all the time I am in my room.
☐	☐	38. I attend almost all the plays that are presented.
☐	☐	39. I prefer reading to attending a football game.
☐	☐	40. I have a personal library of over 50 books in my room, not counting textbooks.
☐	☐	41. I have many friends.
☐	☐	42. I don't like to eat alone.
☐	☐	43. I like hunting and fishing.
☐	☐	44. I would rather play cards or chess than simply sit and read.
☐	☐	45. I have only one or two close friends.

Personal Orientation Test

Answer the following items true or false. Answer every item. It is your opinion that is important. There are no right or wrong answers.

T   F

☐ ☐   1. I like art museums.

☐ ☐   2. I like to exercise just for the fun of it.

☐ ☐   3. Life is a challenge.

☐ ☐   4. I have several items of sport's equipment in my room.

☐ ☐   5. I buy a new book or magazine every week.

☐ ☐   6. I prefer having a roommate to living alone.

☐ ☐   7. I prefer exotic foreign foods to ordinary meals.

☐ ☐   8. I would rather listen to music than play cards.

☐ ☐   9. Participation in sports develops initiative.

☐ ☐ 10. Chess teaches logical thinking and concentration.

☐ ☐ 11. I would rather dine in a good restaurant than go to an informal party.

☐ ☐ 12. Monopoly is more fun than bridge.

☐ ☐ 13. I like intellectual challenges.

☐ ☐ 14. I like the out-of-doors.

☐ ☐ 15. I would rather read than watch TV.

☐ ☐ 16. I prefer studying in the student center to studying in my room.

☐ ☐ 17. I would rather work in a job I enjoy than travel.

☐ ☐ 18. After studying for a while I have to go talk to someone before I can concentrate again.

☐ ☐ 19. I smoke heavily.

☐ ☐ 20. I prefer a ball game to a concert.

☐ ☐ 21. I think Picasso's art is phony.

☐ ☐ 22. I prefer light music to heavy symphonies.

☐ ☐ 23. Card games are a waste of time.

□ □   24. I would rather have wine than milk with a meal.

□ □   25. I know more about foods than most people.

□ □   26. Feeling physically fit is important to me.

□ □   27. Puzzles tend to sharpen your mind.

□ □   28. To do good work in school, it is necessary to be in good physical condition.

□ □   29. I would rather sit in on a bull session than read.

□ □   30. People who play a lot of bridge tend to do poorly in school.

□ □   31. The scent of food is disagreeable to many people.

□ □   32. I would rather grab a quick snack than sit over a long meal in the evening.

□ □   33. The person who enjoys ballet is usually not very well adjusted socially.

□ □   34. Modern art is a reflection of confused minds.

□ □   35. I eat a lot of different kinds of cheeses.

□ □   36. I would rather have steak and potatoes than some kind of foreign food.

□ □   37. I play classical music all the time I am in my room.

□ □   38. I attend almost all the plays that are presented.

□ □   39. I prefer reading to attending a football game.

□ □   40. I have a personal library of over 50 books in my room, not counting textbooks.

□ □   41. I have many friends.

□ □   42. I don't like to eat alone.

□ □   43. I like hunting and fishing.

□ □   44. I would rather play cards or chess than simply sit and read.

□ □   45. I have only one or two close friends.

Personal Orientation Test

Answer the following items true or false. Answer every item. It is your opinion that is important. There are no right or wrong answers.

T   F

☐ ☐   1. I like art museums.

☐ ☐   2. I like to exercise just for the fun of it.

☐ ☐   3. Life is a challenge.

☐ ☐   4. I have several items of sport's equipment in my room.

☐ ☐   5. I buy a new book or magazine every week.

☐ ☐   6. I prefer having a roommate to living alone.

☐ ☐   7. I prefer exotic foreign foods to ordinary meals.

☐ ☐   8. I would rather listen to music than play cards.

☐ ☐   9. Participation in sports develops initiative.

☐ ☐   10. Chess teaches logical thinking and concentration.

☐ ☐   11. I would rather dine in a good restaurant than go to an informal party.

☐ ☐   12. Monopoly is more fun than bridge.

☐ ☐   13. I like intellectual challenges.

☐ ☐   14. I like the out-of-doors.

☐ ☐   15. I would rather read than watch TV.

☐ ☐   16. I prefer studying in the student center to studying in my room.

☐ ☐   17. I would rather work in a job I enjoy than travel.

☐ ☐   18. After studying for a while I have to go talk to someone before I can concentrate again.

☐ ☐   19. I smoke heavily.

☐ ☐   20. I prefer a ball game to a concert.

☐ ☐   21. I think Picasso's art is phony.

☐ ☐   22. I prefer light music to heavy symphonies.

☐ ☐   23. Card games are a waste of time.

T   F

☐ ☐   24. I would rather have wine than milk with a meal.

☐ ☐   25. I know more about foods than most people.

☐ ☐   26. Feeling physically fit is important to me.

☐ ☐   27. Puzzles tend to sharpen your mind.

☐ ☐   28. To do good work in school, it is necessary to be in good physical condition.

☐ ☐   29. I would rather sit in on a bull session than read.

☐ ☐   30. People who play a lot of bridge tend to do poorly in school.

☐ ☐   31. The scent of food is disagreeable to many people.

☐ ☐   32. I would rather grab a quick snack than sit over a long meal in the evening.

☐ ☐   33. The person who enjoys ballet is usually not very well adjusted socially.

☐ ☐   34. Modern art is a reflection of confused minds.

☐ ☐   35. I eat a lot of different kinds of cheeses.

☐ ☐   36. I would rather have steak and potatoes than some kind of foreign food.

☐ ☐   37. I play classical music all the time I am in my room.

☐ ☐   38. I attend almost all the plays that are presented.

☐ ☐   39. I prefer reading to attending a football game.

☐ ☐   40. I have a personal library of over 50 books in my room, not counting textbooks.

☐ ☐   41. I have many friends.

☐ ☐   42. I don't like to eat alone.

☐ ☐   43. I like hunting and fishing.

☐ ☐   44. I would rather play cards or chess than simply sit and read.

☐ ☐   45. I have only one or two close friends.

Personal Orientation Test

Answer the following items true or false. Answer every item. It is your opinion that is important. There are no right or wrong answers.

T   F

☐ ☐   1. I like art museums.

☐ ☐   2. I like to exercise just for the fun of it.

☐ ☐   3. Life is a challenge.

☐ ☐   4. I have several items of sport's equipment in my room.

☐ ☐   5. I buy a new book or magazine every week.

☐ ☐   6. I prefer having a roommate to living alone.

☐ ☐   7. I prefer exotic foreign foods to ordinary meals.

☐ ☐   8. I would rather listen to music than play cards.

☐ ☐   9. Participation in sports develops initiative.

☐ ☐ 10. Chess teaches logical thinking and concentration.

☐ ☐ 11. I would rather dine in a good restaurant than go to an informal party.

☐ ☐ 12. Monopoly is more fun than bridge.

☐ ☐ 13. I like intellectual challenges.

☐ ☐ 14. I like the out-of-doors.

☐ ☐ 15. I would rather read than watch TV.

☐ ☐ 16. I prefer studying in the student center to studying in my room.

☐ ☐ 17. I would rather work in a job I enjoy than travel.

☐ ☐ 18. After studying for a while I have to go talk to someone before I can concentrate again.

☐ ☐ 19. I smoke heavily.

☐ ☐ 20. I prefer a ball game to a concert.

☐ ☐ 21. I think Picasso's art is phony.

☐ ☐ 22. I prefer light music to heavy symphonies.

☐ ☐ 23. Card games are a waste of time.

☐ ☐   24. I would rather have wine than milk with a meal.

☐ ☐   25. I know more about foods than most people.

☐ ☐   26. Feeling physically fit is important to me.

☐ ☐   27. Puzzles tend to sharpen your mind.

☐ ☐   28. To do good work in school, it is necessary to be in good physical condition.

☐ ☐   29. I would rather sit in on a bull session than read.

☐ ☐   30. People who play a lot of bridge tend to do poorly in school.

☐ ☐   31. The scent of food is disagreeable to many people.

☐ ☐   32. I would rather grab a quick snack than sit over a long meal in the evening.

☐ ☐   33. The person who enjoys ballet is usually not very well adjusted socially.

☐ ☐   34. Modern art is a reflection of confused minds.

☐ ☐   35. I eat a lot of different kinds of cheeses.

☐ ☐   36. I would rather have steak and potatoes than some kind of foreign food.

☐ ☐   37. I play classical music all the time I am in my room.

☐ ☐   38. I attend almost all the plays that are presented.

☐ ☐   39. I prefer reading to attending a football game.

☐ ☐   40. I have a personal library of over 50 books in my room, not counting textbooks.

☐ ☐   41. I have many friends.

☐ ☐   42. I don't like to eat alone.

☐ ☐   43. I like hunting and fishing.

☐ ☐   44. I would rather play cards or chess than simply sit and read.

☐ ☐   45. I have only one or two close friends.

Personal Orientation Test

Answer the following items true or false. Answer every item. It is your opinion that is important. There are no right or wrong answers.

T F

☐ ☐ 1. I like art museums.

☐ ☐ 2. I like to exercise just for the fun of it.

☐ ☐ 3. Life is a challenge.

☐ ☐ 4. I have several items of sport's equipment in my room.

☐ ☐ 5. I buy a new book or magazine every week.

☐ ☐ 6. I prefer having a roommate to living alone.

☐ ☐ 7. I prefer exotic foreign foods to ordinary meals.

☐ ☐ 8. I would rather listen to music than play cards.

☐ ☐ 9. Participation in sports develops initiative.

☐ ☐ 10. Chess teaches logical thinking and concentration.

☐ ☐ 11. I would rather dine in a good restaurant than go to an informal party.

☐ ☐ 12. Monopoly is more fun than bridge.

☐ ☐ 13. I like intellectual challenges.

☐ ☐ 14. I like the out-of-doors.

☐ ☐ 15. I would rather read than watch TV.

☐ ☐ 16. I prefer studying in the student center to studying in my room.

☐ ☐ 17. I would rather work in a job I enjoy than travel.

☐ ☐ 18. After studying for a while I have to go talk to someone before I can concentrate again.

☐ ☐ 19. I smoke heavily.

☐ ☐ 20. I prefer a ball game to a concert.

☐ ☐ 21. I think Picasso's art is phony.

☐ ☐ 22. I prefer light music to heavy symphonies.

☐ ☐ 23. Card games are a waste of time.

T   F

☐   ☐   24. I would rather have wine than milk with a meal.

☐   ☐   25. I know more about foods than most people.

☐   ☐   26. Feeling physically fit is important to me.

☐   ☐   27. Puzzles tend to sharpen your mind.

☐   ☐   28. To do good work in school, it is necessary to be in good physical condition.

☐   ☐   29. I would rather sit in on a bull session than read.

☐   ☐   30. People who play a lot of bridge tend to do poorly in school.

☐   ☐   31. The scent of food is disagreeable to many people.

☐   ☐   32. I would rather grab a quick snack than sit over a long meal in the evening.

☐   ☐   33. The person who enjoys ballet is usually not very well adjusted socially.

☐   ☐   34. Modern art is a reflection of confused minds.

☐   ☐   35. I eat a lot of different kinds of cheeses.

☐   ☐   36. I would rather have steak and potatoes than some kind of foreign food.

☐   ☐   37. I play classical music all the time I am in my room.

☐   ☐   38. I attend almost all the plays that are presented.

☐   ☐   39. I prefer reading to attending a football game.

☐   ☐   40. I have a personal library of over 50 books in my room, not counting textbooks.

☐   ☐   41. I have many friends.

☐   ☐   42. I don't like to eat alone.

☐   ☐   43. I like hunting and fishing.

☐   ☐   44. I would rather play cards or chess than simply sit and read.

☐   ☐   45. I have only one or two close friends.

Examinee ———————————————————————————————————————
Examiner ———————————————————————————————————————

Personal Orientation Test

Answer the following items true or false. Answer every item. It is your opinion that is important. There are no right or wrong answers.

T   F

☐   ☐   1. I like art museums.

☐   ☐   2. I like to exercise just for the fun of it.

☐   ☐   3. Life is a challenge.

☐   ☐   4. I have several items of sport's equipment in my room.

☐   ☐   5. I buy a new book or magazine every week.

☐   ☐   6. I prefer having a roommate to living alone.

☐   ☐   7. I prefer exotic foreign foods to ordinary meals.

☐   ☐   8. I would rather listen to music than play cards.

☐   ☐   9. Participation in sports develops initiative.

☐   ☐   10. Chess teaches logical thinking and concentration.

☐   ☐   11. I would rather dine in a good restaurant than go to an informal party.

☐   ☐   12. Monopoly is more fun than bridge.

☐   ☐   13. I like intellectual challenges.

☐   ☐   14. I like the out-of-doors.

☐   ☐   15. I would rather read than watch TV.

☐   ☐   16. I prefer studying in the student center to studying in my room.

☐   ☐   17. I would rather work in a job I enjoy than travel.

☐   ☐   18. After studying for a while I have to go talk to someone before I can concentrate again.

☐   ☐   19. I smoke heavily.

☐   ☐   20. I prefer a ball game to a concert.

☐   ☐   21. I think Picasso's art is phony.

☐   ☐   22. I prefer light music to heavy symphonies.

☐   ☐   23. Card games are a waste of time.

☐ ☐ 24. I would rather have wine than milk with a meal.

☐ ☐ 25. I know more about foods than most people.

☐ ☐ 26. Feeling physically fit is important to me.

☐ ☐ 27. Puzzles tend to sharpen your mind.

☐ ☐ 28. To do good work in school, it is necessary to be in good physical condition.

☐ ☐ 29. I would rather sit in on a bull session than read.

☐ ☐ 30. People who play a lot of bridge tend to do poorly in school.

☐ ☐ 31. The scent of food is disagreeable to many people.

☐ ☐ 32. I would rather grab a quick snack than sit over a long meal in the evening.

☐ ☐ 33. The person who enjoys ballet is usually not very well adjusted socially.

☐ ☐ 34. Modern art is a reflection of confused minds.

☐ ☐ 35. I eat a lot of different kinds of cheeses.

☐ ☐ 36. I would rather have steak and potatoes than some kind of foreign food.

☐ ☐ 37. I play classical music all the time I am in my room.

☐ ☐ 38. I attend almost all the plays that are presented.

☐ ☐ 39. I prefer reading to attending a football game.

☐ ☐ 40. I have a personal library of over 50 books in my room, not counting textbooks.

☐ ☐ 41. I have many friends.

☐ ☐ 42. I don't like to eat alone.

☐ ☐ 43. I like hunting and fishing.

☐ ☐ 44. I would rather play cards or chess than simply sit and read.

☐ ☐ 45. I have only one or two close friends.

Examinee _____

Examiner _____

Personal Orientation Test

Answer the following items true or false. Answer every item. It is your opinion that is important. There are no right or wrong answers.

T   F

☐ ☐   1. I like art museums.

☐ ☐   2. I like to exercise just for the fun of it.

☐ ☐   3. Life is a challenge.

☐ ☐   4. I have several items of sport's equipment in my room.

☐ ☐   5. I buy a new book or magazine every week.

☐ ☐   6. I prefer having a roommate to living alone.

☐ ☐   7. I prefer exotic foreign foods to ordinary meals.

☐ ☐   8. I would rather listen to music than play cards.

☐ ☐   9. Participation in sports develops initiative.

☐ ☐   10. Chess teaches logical thinking and concentration.

☐ ☐   11. I would rather dine in a good restaurant than go to an informal party.

☐ ☐   12. Monopoly is more fun than bridge.

☐ ☐   13. I like intellectual challenges.

☐ ☐   14. I like the out-of-doors.

☐ ☐   15. I would rather read than watch TV.

☐ ☐   16. I prefer studying in the student center to studying in my room.

☐ ☐   17. I would rather work in a job I enjoy than travel.

☐ ☐   18. After studying for a while I have to go talk to someone before I can concentrate again.

☐ ☐   19. I smoke heavily.

☐ ☐   20. I prefer a ball game to a concert.

☐ ☐   21. I think Picasso's art is phony.

☐ ☐   22. I prefer light music to heavy symphonies.

☐ ☐   23. Card games are a waste of time.

☐   ☐   24. I would rather have wine than milk with a meal.

☐   ☐   25. I know more about foods than most people.

☐   ☐   26. Feeling physically fit is important to me.

☐   ☐   27. Puzzles tend to sharpen your mind.

☐   ☐   28. To do good work in school, it is necessary to be in good physical condition.

☐   ☐   29. I would rather sit in on a bull session than read.

☐   ☐   30. People who play a lot of bridge tend to do poorly in school.

☐   ☐   31. The scent of food is disagreeable to many people.

☐   ☐   32. I would rather grab a quick snack than sit over a long meal in the evening.

☐   ☐   33. The person who enjoys ballet is usually not very well adjusted socially.

☐   ☐   34. Modern art is a reflection of confused minds.

☐   ☐   35. I eat a lot of different kinds of cheeses.

☐   ☐   36. I would rather have steak and potatoes than some kind of foreign food.

☐   ☐   37. I play classical music all the time I am in my room.

☐   ☐   38. I attend almost all the plays that are presented.

☐   ☐   39. I prefer reading to attending a football game.

☐   ☐   40. I have a personal library of over 50 books in my room, not counting textbooks.

☐   ☐   41. I have many friends.

☐   ☐   42. I don't like to eat alone.

☐   ☐   43. I like hunting and fishing.

☐   ☐   44. I would rather play cards or chess than simply sit and read.

☐   ☐   45. I have only one or two close friends.

Personal Orientation Test

Answer the following items true or false. Answer every item. It is your opinion that is important. There are no right or wrong answers.

T   F

☐ ☐   1. I like art museums.

☐ ☐   2. I like to exercise just for the fun of it.

☐ ☐   3. Life is a challenge.

☐ ☐   4. I have several items of sport's equipment in my room.

☐ ☐   5. I buy a new book or magazine every week.

☐ ☐   6. I prefer having a roommate to living alone.

☐ ☐   7. I prefer exotic foreign foods to ordinary meals.

☐ ☐   8. I would rather listen to music than play cards.

☐ ☐   9. Participation in sports develops initiative.

☐ ☐   10. Chess teaches logical thinking and concentration.

☐ ☐   11. I would rather dine in a good restaurant than go to an informal party.

☐ ☐   12. Monopoly is more fun than bridge.

☐ ☐   13. I like intellectual challenges.

☐ ☐   14. I like the out-of-doors.

☐ ☐   15. I would rather read than watch TV.

☐ ☐   16. I prefer studying in the student center to studying in my room.

☐ ☐   17. I would rather work in a job I enjoy than travel.

☐ ☐   18. After studying for a while I have to go talk to someone before I can concentrate again.

☐ ☐   19. I smoke heavily.

☐ ☐   20. I prefer a ball game to a concert.

☐ ☐   21. I think Picasso's art is phony.

☐ ☐   22. I prefer light music to heavy symphonies.

☐ ☐   23. Card games are a waste of time.

T   F

☐ ☐   24. I would rather have wine than milk with a meal.

☐ ☐   25. I know more about foods than most people.

☐ ☐   26. Feeling physically fit is important to me.

☐ ☐   27. Puzzles tend to sharpen your mind.

☐ ☐   28. To do good work in school, it is necessary to be in good physical condition.

☐ ☐   29. I would rather sit in on a bull session than read.

☐ ☐   30. People who play a lot of bridge tend to do poorly in school.

☐ ☐   31. The scent of food is disagreeable to many people.

☐ ☐   32. I would rather grab a quick snack than sit over a long meal in the evening.

☐ ☐   33. The person who enjoys ballet is usually not very well adjusted socially.

☐ ☐   34. Modern art is a reflection of confused minds.

☐ ☐   35. I eat a lot of different kinds of cheeses.

☐ ☐   36. I would rather have steak and potatoes than some kind of foreign food.

☐ ☐   37. I play classical music all the time I am in my room.

☐ ☐   38. I attend almost all the plays that are presented.

☐ ☐   39. I prefer reading to attending a football game.

☐ ☐   40. I have a personal library of over 50 books in my room, not counting textbooks.

☐ ☐   41. I have many friends.

☐ ☐   42. I don't like to eat alone.

☐ ☐   43. I like hunting and fishing.

☐ ☐   44. I would rather play cards or chess than simply sit and read.

☐ ☐   45. I have only one or two close friends.

Personal Orientation Test

Test Profile

%ile	Ga	Sp	Go	Ae	So	S.A.	U.R.	%ile
98	––	––	––	––	––	––	––	98
96	–	–	–	–	–	–	–	96
94	–	–	–	–	–	–	–	94
92	–	–	–	–	–	–	–	92
88	–	–	–	–	–	–	–	88
84	––	––	––	––	––	––	––	84
79	–	–	–	–	–	–	–	79
73	–	–	–	–	–	–	–	73
66	–	–	–	–	–	–	–	66
58	–	–	–	–	–	–	–	58
50								50
42	–	–	–	–	–	–	–	42
34	–	–	–	–	–	–	–	34
28	–	–	–	–	–	–	–	28
21	–	–	–	–	–	–	–	21
16	––	––	––	––	––	––	––	16
11	–	–	–	–	–	–	–	11
8	–	–	–	–	–	–	–	8
6	–	–	–	–	–	–	–	6
4	–	–	–	–	–	–	–	4
2	––	––	––	––	––	––	––	2

Test Interpretation

Examinee _____ Age_____ Sex_____
Examiner _____

Personal Orientation Test

Test Profile

%ile	Ga	Sp	Go	Ae	So	S.A.	U.R.	%ile
98	--	--	--	--	--	--	--	98
96	-	-	-	-	-	-	-	96
94	-	-	-	-	-	-	-	94
92	-	-	-	-	-	-	-	92
88	-	-	-	-	-	-	-	88
84	--	--	--	--	--	--	--	84
79	-	-	-	-	-	-	-	79
73	-	-	-	-	-	-	-	73
66	-	-	-	-	-	-	-	66
58	-	-	-	-	-	-	-	58
50								50
42	-	-	-	-	-	-	-	42
34	-	-	-	-	-	-	-	34
28	-	-	-	-	-	-	-	28
21	-	-	-	-	-	-	-	21
16	--	--	--	--	--	--	--	16
11	-	-	-	-	-	-	-	11
8	-	-	-	-	-	-	-	8
6	-	-	-	-	-	-	-	6
4	-	-	-	-	-	-	-	4
2	--	--	--	--	--	--	--	2

Test Interpretation

Examinee _____ Age_____ Sex_____

Examiner _____

Personal Orientation Test

Test Profile

%ile	Ga	Sp	Go	Ae	So	S.A.	U.R.	%ile
98	--	--	--	--	--	--	--	98
96	-	-	-	-	-	-	-	96
94	-	-	-	-	-	-	-	94
92	-	-	-	-	-	-	-	92
88	-	-	-	-	-	-	-	88
84	--	--	--	--	--	--	--	84
79	-	-	-	-	-	-	-	79
73	-	-	-	-	-	-	-	73
66	-	-	-	-	-	-	-	66
58	-	-	-	-	-	-	-	58
50								50
42	-	-	-	-	-	-	-	42
34	-	-	-	-	-	-	-	34
28	-	-	-	-	-	-	-	28
21	-	-	-	-	-	-	-	21
16	--	--	--	--	--	--	--	16
11	-	-	-	-	-	-	-	11
8	-	-	-	-	-	-	-	8
6	-	-	-	-	-	-	-	6
4	-	-	-	-	-	-	-	4
2	--	--	--	--	--	--	--	2

Test Interpretation

Examinee _____ Age_____ Sex_____

Examiner _____

Personal Orientation Test

Test Profile

%ile	Ga	Sp	Go	Ae	So	S.A.	U.R.	%ile
98	---	---	---	---	---	---	---	98
96	–	–	–	–	–	–	–	96
94	–	–	–	–	–	–	–	94
92	–	–	–	–	–	–	–	92
88	–	–	–	–	–	–	–	88
84	---	---	---	---	---	---	---	84
79	–	–	–	–	–	–	–	79
73	–	–	–	–	–	–	–	73
66	–	–	–	–	–	–	–	66
58	–	–	–	–	–	–	–	58
50								50
42	–	–	–	–	–	–	–	42
34	–	–	–	–	–	–	–	34
28	–	–	–	–	–	–	–	28
21	–	–	–	–	–	–	–	21
16	---	---	---	---	---	---	---	16
11	–	–	–	–	–	–	–	11
8	–	–	–	–	–	–	–	8
6	–	–	–	–	–	–	–	6
4	–	–	–	–	–	–	–	4
2	---	---	---	---	---	---	---	2

Test Interpretation

Personal Orientation Test

Test Profile

%ile	Ga	Sp	Go	Ae	So	S.A.	U.R.	%ile
98	––	––	––	––	––	––	––	98
96	–	–	–	–	–	–	–	96
94	–	–	–	–	–	–	–	94
92	–	–	–	–	–	–	–	92
88	–	–	–	–	–	–	––	88
84	––	––	––	––	––	––	––	84
79	–	–	–	–	–	–	–	79
73	–	–	–	–	–	–	–	73
66	–	–	–	–	–	–	–	66
58	–	–	–	–	–	–	–	58
50								50
42	–	–	–	–	–	–	–	42
34	–	–	–	–	–	–	–	34
28	–	–	–	–	–	–	–	28
21	–	–	–	–	–	–	–	21
16	––	––	––	––	––	––	––	16
11	–	–	–	–	–	–	–	11
8	–	–	–	–	–	–	–	8
6	–	–	–	–	–	–	–	6
4	–	–	–	–	–	–	–	4
2	––	––	––	––	––	––	––	2

Test Interpretation

Personal Orientation Test

Test Profile

%ile	Ga	Sp	Go	Ae	So	S.A.	U.R.	%ile
98	--	--	--	--	--	--	--	98
96	-	-	-	-	-	-	-	96
94	-	-	-	-	-	-	-	94
92	-	-	-	-	-	-	-	92
88	-	-	-	-	-	-	-	88
84	--	--	--	--	--	--	--	84
79	-	-	-	-	-	-	-	79
73	-	-	-	-	-	-	-	73
66	-	-	-	-	-	-	-	66
58	-	-	-	-	-	-	-	58
50								50
42	-	-	-	-	-	-	-	42
34	-	-	-	-	-	-	-	34
28	-	-	-	-	-	-	-	28
21	-	-	-	-	-	-	-	21
16	--	--	--	--	--	--	--	16
11	-	-	-	-	-	-	-	11
8	-	-	-	-	-	-	-	8
6	-	-	-	-	-	-	-	6
4	-	-	-	-	-	-	-	4
2	--	--	--	--	--	--	--	2

Test Interpretation

Personal Orientation Test

Test Profile

%ile	Ga	Sp	Go	Ae	So	S.A.	U.R.	%ile
98	--	--	--	--	--	--	--	98
96	-	-	-	-	-	-	-	96
94	-	-	-	-	-	-	-	94
92	-	-	-	-	-	-	-	92
88	-	-	-	-	-	-	-	88
84	--	--	--	--	--	--	--	84
79	-	-	-	-	-	-	-	79
73	-	-	-	-	-	-	-	73
66	-	-	-	-	-	-	-	66
58	-	-	-	-	-	-	-	58
50								50
42	-	-	-	-	-	-	-	42
34	-	-	-	-	-	-	-	34
28	-	-	-	-	-	-	-	28
21	-	-	-	-	-	-	-	21
16	--	--	--	--	--	--	--	16
11	-	-	-	-	-	-	-	11
8	-	-	-	-	-	-	-	8
6	-	-	-	-	-	-	-	6
4	-	-	-	-	-	-	-	4
2	--	--	--	--	--	--	--	2

Test Interpretation

183

Examinee _____ Age_____ Sex_____

Examiner _____

Personal Orientation Test

Test Profile

%ile	Ga	Sp	Go	Ae	So	S.A.	U.R.	%ile
98	--	--	--	--	--	--	--	98
96	-	-	-	-	-	-	-	96
94	-	-	-	-	-	-	-	94
92	-	-	-	-	-	-	-	92
88	-	-	-	-	-	-	-	88
84	--	--	--	--	--	--	--	84
79	-	-	-	-	-	-	-	79
73	-	-	-	-	-	-	-	73
66	-	-	-	-	-	-	-	66
58	-	-	-	-	-	-	-	58
50								50
42	-	-	-	-	-	-	-	42
34	-	-	-	-	-	-	-	34
28	-	-	-	-	-	-	-	28
21	-	-	-	-	-	-	-	21
16	--	--	--	--	--	--	--	16
11	-	-	-	-	-	-	-	11
8	-	-	-	-	-	-	-	8
6	-	-	-	-	-	-	-	6
4	-	-	-	-	-	-	-	4
2	--	--	--	--	--	--	--	2

Test Interpretation

185

Personal Orientation Test

Test Profile

%ile	Ga	Sp	Go	Ae	So	S.A.	U.R.	%ile
98	--	--	--	--	--	--	--	98
96	–	–	–	–	–	–	–	96
.94	–	–	–	–	–	–	–	94
92	–	–	–	–	–	–	–	92
88	–	–	–	–	–	–	–	88
84	--	--	--	--	--	--	--	84
79	–	–	–	–	–	–	–	79
73	–	–	–	–	–	–	–	73
66	–	–	–	–	–	–	–	66
58	–	–	–	–	–	–	–	58
50								50
42	–	–	–	–	–	–	–	42
34	–	–	–	–	–	–	–	34
28	–	–	–	–	–	–	–	28
21	–	–	–	–	–	–	–	21
16	--	--	--	--	--	--	--	16
11	–	–	–	–	–	–	–	11
8	–	–	–	–	–	–	–	8
6	–	–	–	–	–	–	–	6
4	–	–	–	–	–	–	–	4
2	--	--	--	--	--	--	--	2

Test Interpretation

Personal Orientation Test

Test Profile

%ile	Ga	Sp	Go	Ae	So	S.A.	U.R.	%ile
98	--	--	--	--	--	--	--	98
96	-	-	-	-	-	-	-	96
94	-	-	-	-	-	-	-	94
92	-	-	-	-	-	-	-	92
88	-	-	-	-	-	-	-	88
84	--	--	--	--	--	--	--	84
79	-	-	-	-	-	-	-	79
73	-	-	-	-	-	-	-	73
66	-	-	-	-	-	-	-	66
58	-	-	-	-	-	-	-	58
50								50
42	-	-	-	-	-	-	-	42
34	-	-	-	-	-	-	-	34
28	-	-	-	-	-	-	-	28
21	-	-	-	-	-	-	-	21
16	--	--	--	--	--	--	--	16
11	-	-	-	-	-	-	-	11
8	-	-	-	-	-	-	-	8
6	-	-	-	-	-	-	-	6
4	-	-	-	-	-	-	-	4
2	--	--	--	--	--	--	--	2

Test Interpretation

Examinee ——————————————————————— Age———— Sex————

Examiner ——————————————————————————————————

Personal Orientation Test

Test Profile

%ile	Ga	Sp	Go	Ae	So	S.A.	U.R.	%ile
98	--	--	--	--	--	--	--	98
96	-	-	-	-	-	-	-	96
94	-	-	-	-	-	-	-	94
92	-	-	-	-	-	-	-	92
88	-	-	-	-	-	-	-	88
84	--	--	--	--	--	--	--	84
79	-	-	-	-	-	-	-	79
73	-	-	-	-	-	-	-	73
66	-	-	-	-	-	-	-	66
58	-	-	-	-	-	-	-	58
50								50
42	-	-	-	-	-	-	-	42
34	-	-	-	-	-	-	-	34
28	-	-	-	-	-	-	-	28
21	-	-	-	-	-	-	-	21
16	--	--	--	--	--	--	--	16
11	-	-	-	-	-	-	-	11
8	-	-	-	-	-	-	-	8
6	-	-	-	-	-	-	-	6
4	-	-	-	-	-	-	-	4
2	--	--	--	--	--	--	--	2

Test Interpretation

Examinee _____ Age_____ Sex_____

Examiner _____

Personal Orientation Test

Test Profile

%ile	Ga	Sp	Go	Ae	So	S.A.	U.R.	%ile
98	––	––	––	––	––	––	––	98
96	–	–	–	–	–	–	–	96
94	–	–	–	–	–	–	–	94
92	–	–	–	–	–	–	–	92
88	–	–	–	–	–	–	–	88
84	––	––	––	––	––	––	––	84
79	–	–	–	–	–	–	–	79
73	–	–	–	–	–	–	–	73
66	–	–	–	–	–	–	–	66
58	–	–	–	–	–	–	–	58
50								50
42	–	–	–	–	–	–	–	42
34	–	–	–	–	–	–	–	34
28	–	–	–	–	–	–	–	28
21	–	–	–	–	–	–	–	21
16	––	––	––	––	––	––	––	16
11	–	–	–	–	–	–	–	11
8	–	–	–	–	–	–	–	8
6	–	–	–	–	–	–	–	6
4	–	–	–	–	–	–	–	4
2	––	––	––	––	––	––	––	2

Test Interpretation

193

LABORATORY EXERCISE 11

Cross-Validation of the POT

PURPOSE

This exercise allows the class to cross-validate the scales of the POT. Using the scoring keys prepared in Exercise 10, the test is scored for the second individual in each of the criterion groups and for another person in the students-in-general group. If the majority of criterion group scores higher than the general group on their own scale, there is some indication the scale "holds up" in cross-validation. For example, we would expect the "gaming" group to score higher on the "gaming" scale than the students-in-general group.

CROSS-VALIDATION

Items for the POT scales were selected on the basis of a difference in percentage of responses in the criterion and general student groups. It could be that these differences were due to chance alone. It could be that validity was found because random effects gave the differences. The process of checking this possibility is the process of cross-validation. Cross-validation involves choosing a new group of subjects, both criterion and general groups in this exercise, to confirm the original findings. In certain cases, it is especially critical that the results are cross-validated: when a small number of subjects are used, when relatively few items have been selected from an initially large pool of items, and when no specific hypotheses have been formulated in the initial development of the item pool. In all cases of validation, the results should be evaluated by some method of cross-validation.

CROSS-VALIDATION OF POT

1. Using the scales constructed in Exercise 10, the class members should score the test of the second individual who, in their opinion, belonged in each of the criterion groups. The test for the second "gaming" person should be scored on the "gaming" scale; the test for the "sporting" person should be scored on the "sporting" scale, etc.
2. The test for a second students-in-general group person should be scored on all five scales. These scores will provide a basis of comparison for the cross-validation sample of subjects.
3. The percentile equivalents of these raw scores should be found in the norm tables in Exercise 10. In each case, the student should identify whether the score is above or below the median (50th percentile).
4. The class then determines how many "gaming" individuals in the cross-validation sample scored above and below the median of the gaming scale and how many in the second general-group sample scored above and below the median. These numbers should be entered in Table 11.1.
5. The same process is carried out for the remaining cross-validation and general-group samples. The numbers scoring above and below the median should be recorded in Tables 11.2–11.5.
6. If there are more criterion group papers above the median than general group papers, the test can be considered to be cross-validated. A statistical test of whether the scale has cross-validated is χ^2.

$$\chi^2 = \frac{N(ad - bc)^2}{(a + b)(c + d)(a + c)(b + d)}$$

where the letters refer to the numbers in the cells of the table. $N = a + b + c + d$.

7. If χ^2 is greater than 5.99 (found in a table of critical values for χ^2), we can say that there are only 5 chances in 100 that the results were due to chance. In ·other words, the scale has held up in cross-validation.

SUGGESTED READINGS

Anastasi, A. *Psychological Testing* (4th ed.). New York: Macmillan, 1976, pp. 219–221.

Brown, F. G., *Principles of Educational and Psychological Testing* (2nd ed.). New York: Holt, Rinehart and Winston, 1976, p. 118.

Cronbach, L. J. *Essentials of Psychological Testing* (3rd ed.). New York: Harper & Row, 1970, pp. 433–434.

Name _____

Table 11.1 Gaming

Group	Below Median	Above Median
Gaming	a	b
Students-in-General	c	d

Table 11.2 Sporting

Group	Below Median	Above Median
Sporting	a	b
Students-in-General	c	d

Table 11.3 Gourmet

Group	Below Median	Above Median
Gourmet	a	b
Students-in-General	c	d

Table 11.4 Aesthetic

Group	Below Median	Above Median
Aesthetic	a	b
Students-in-General	c	d

Table 11.5 Social

Group	Below Median	Above Median
Social	a	b
Students-in-General	c	d

Name _____

Assignment for **EXERCISE 11**

1. Score a second subject in each criterion category (the cross-validation samples) and a second students-in-general subject. Find percentile equivalents from norm tables.
2. Tabulate numbers in Tables 11.1–11.5.
3. Calculate the χ^2 values and compare with the critical value.
4. Answer the following questions:
   a. Why is cross-validation important?

   b. What are three possible reasons why certain scales did not cross-validate (assuming some did not)?

LABORATORY EXERCISE 12

Administration and Scoring of a Projective Test: The Picture Interpretation Test

PURPOSE

This exercise gives the student a chance to administer and score a projective test. Comparisons are made with the Personal Orientation Test measuring the same characteristics.

PROJECTIVE TESTS

A projective test typically consists of a set of ambiguous stimulus materials that are presented to the subject. The individual is asked to use imagination to describe what the materials suggest or to tell a story about them. The subject must project meaning on the test materials; the kind of story told or the kind of description given can be used to evaluate personality characteristics or needs and drives. While almost any material could be used for a projective test, the kind of material determines the responses that the subject is required to make. Thus, the Rorschach Test consists of a series of ambiguous ink blots and the subject is asked to describe these blots. The Rorschach is used to assess the way a person views and deals with the world. As with any of the projective tests, the scoring is extremely subtle and requires extensive training. The Thematic Apperception Test (TAT) consists of pictures, some with great clarity of detail and some vague, about which the subject must make up a story. These responses are used to evaluate the needs and drives of the subject.

PICTURE INTERPRETATION TEST

The Picture Interpretation Test (PIT) is similar to the TAT in type of material; however, the subject is asked to respond somewhat differently. The PIT consists of three pictures which the subject is asked to describe. We have selected materials for the Picture Interpretation Test that encourage the subject to respond in ways that can be used to assess characteristics on the dimensions that have been already validated on the Personal Orientation Test. This has been done so that the two tests can be compared.

All tests are, to some extent, projective. That is, the subject projects meaning on the situation and responds in terms of the way he or she understands the item. The empirically derived tests, however, differ from the usual projective tests in that scoring of the former is based on items demonstrated to differ between two groups. Why the item responses of the two groups differ is not of critical importance. The usual approach to scoring of a projective test is based on a theory of how the test works. From that theory, the meaning of a particular response can be predicted.

In the case of Rorschach and TAT, the tests have been in use for many years, and a great deal of research has been done on both tests. Some types of responses have been shown to be valid indicators of different facets of adjustment. Other responses, which according to the theory of the tests should have predicted a particular personality characteristic, have not worked out. The well-trained examiner who uses the test knows these research findings and takes them into account in interpreting the results.

In using this projective test, there is no evidence that the test is valid as a measure of personal orientation. The only basis for scoring the test is the theory about how it should work.

The theory of the Picture Interpretation Test is that an individual with a particular orientation will respond to those aspects of the picture that are most meaningful. The gaming person will note the games involved and will include them in reporting what is going on. The sporting equipment or the food may be ignored. On the other hand, the gourmet individual will notice the food and include it, but may not notice the sporting equipment, or may not include it in the story. Included in the theory is the idea that people will notice first those things that are closest to their orientation and that the main theme of the story will be based on the kinds of things that are important to them. Along the same lines, if a person ignores a prominent aspect of the picture, this might suggest a total lack of interest. Furthermore, including something in the situation that is not present in the scene might indicate its importance to the subject.

Although there is no direct evidence for the validity of the test, it does show how a projective test is given and illustrates some of the problems of scoring.

In giving the test, you have to accurately record the subject's responses without influencing the person in any way. Later, in scoring, you will have to examine those responses in detail, considering the many different meanings of each response in order to decide how to score the test. If you have been able to give the test to two of the people who took the Personal Orientation Test, you can then look at their responses and your scores to see if you can find evidence that the test does indicate personal orientation.

PROCEDURE

The student should administer the PIT to three individuals. Show the person each picture and read the instructions on the Test Protocol. As the person describes each picture, take extensive notes. Write down specific things the person says. Do not rely on your memory.

SUGGESTED READINGS

Anastasi, A. *Psychological Testing* (4th ed.). New York: Macmillan, 1976, pp. 565–569, 576–585.

Brown, F. G. *Principles of Educational and Psychological Testing* (2nd ed.). New York: Holt, Rinehart and Winston, 1976, pp. 393–401.

Cronbach, L. J. *Essentials of Psychological Testing* (3rd ed.). New York: Harper & Row, 1970, pp. 651–654.

Gronlund, N. E. *Measurement and Evaluation in Teaching* (3rd ed.). New York: Macmillan, 1976, p. 470.

Mehrens, W. A., and Lehmann, I. J. *Measurement and Evaluation in Education and Psychology* (2nd ed.). New York: Holt, Rinehart and Winston, 1975, pp. 580–581.

Thorndike, R. L., and Hagan, E. *Measurement and Evaluation in Psychology and Education* (4th ed.). New York: Wiley, 1977, pp. 498–501.

Test Protocol: Picture Interpretation Test

Directions: I am going to hand you some pictures. I would like you to describe each picture to me and then make up a story about the picture. Tell me what led up to the situation pictured, what the persons in the picture are doing, and what they are going to do next.

Card I

Card II

Card III

Scoring Summary: Picture Interpretation Test

Card I   Primacy   Importance   Additions   Unnoted

Card II   Primacy   Importance   Additions   Unnoted

Card III   Primacy   Importance   Additions   Unnoted

Total Scoring   Ga   Sp   Go   Ae   So

Observations During Testing

Interpretation

210

Examinee ———
Examiner ———

Test Protocol: Picture Interpretation Test

Directions: I am going to hand you some pictures. I would like you to describe each picture to me and then make up a story about the picture. Tell me what led up to the situation pictured, what the persons in the picture are doing, and what they are going to do next.

Card I

Card II

Card III

Scoring Summary: Picture Interpretation Test

Card I   Primacy   Importance   Additions   Unnoted

Card II   Primacy   Importance   Additions   Unnoted

Card III   Primacy   Importance   Additions   Unnoted

Total Scoring   Ga   Sp   Go   Ae   So

Observations During Testing

Interpretation

Test Protocol: Picture Interpretation Test

Directions: I am going to hand you some pictures. I would like you to describe each picture to me and then make up a story about the picture. Tell me what led up to the situation pictured, what the persons in the picture are doing, and what they are going to do next.

Card I

Card II

Card III

Scoring Summary: Picture Interpretation Test

Card I   Primacy   Importance   Additions   Unnoted

Card II   Primacy   Importance   Additions   Unnoted

Card III   Primacy   Importance   Additions   Unnoted

Total Scoring   Ga   Sp   Go   Ae   So

Observations During Testing

Interpretation

Scoring the Picture Interpretation Test

The following scales are to be scored:

Gaming: *Indications in the description or story of materials relating to games.* Reference to physical objects in the picture such as playing cards, the checkerboard, or other games would indicate projection of a gaming orientation. Reference to the behavior or intentions of the individuals in the pictures with respect to gaming would also indicate a projection of this orientation.

Sporting: *Indications in the description or story of materials relating to athletics.* Mention of physical objects in the pictures which are used in athletics or reference to the behavior or motives of individuals in the picture as relating to athletics would indicate the projections of a sporting person.

Gourmet: *Indications in the description or story of materials relating to fine foods and beverages.* Reference to foods and beverages in the pictures or the behavior or intentions of the pictured individuals with respect to eating or drinking fine foods or beverages would indicate a projection of the gourmet orientation.

Aesthetic: *Indications in the description or story of materials relating to the fine arts.* Reference to paintings, sculptured objects, radios or tape recorders, or the artistic design of the furniture pictured would indicate an aesthetic orientation. Mention of the behavior or intentions of the pictured individuals as being oriented toward the fine arts would indicate the projection of an aesthetic orientation.

Social: *Indications in the description or story of materials relating to social activities.* References to bull sessions, parties, social gatherings in general, or other types of interpersonal behavior would indicate this orientation.

Primacy: What aspects of the picture are noted first in describing the story? If several things are mentioned, which can be assumed to be the first noticed by the subject? Scoring of primacy is accomplished by indicating by abbreviation the primary characteristic notice by the subject in the space marked "primacy."

Importance: What is the main theme of the story? What does it center around? If one or more characteristics are predominant, they are indicated with abbreviation, followed by an exclamation point. Characteristics of secondary importance are indicated by abbreviation only. Casual mention is indicated by abbreviation with a circle around it. The following are a few examples of main themes in relation to the five orientations.

A response to Card I such as "The table has just been used for a game of cards" or to Card II such as "The boy is about to engage in a game of checkers" are both indicative of gaming as an important orientation.

Emphasis on the skis in Card I or the tennis racket, gloves, and ball in Card II, in relation to the use of this equipment in a sport, would indicate sporting as a main theme.

The aesthetic orientation as a main theme would be typified by responses such as "The painting and the fireplace make this a beautiful and pleasant scene" (Card I) or "The people are listening to classical music while studying" (Card III).

Emphasis on the wine bottle along with a response such as "A fine meal has been concluded and after dinner wine or brandy was served" would indicate the importance of the gourmet orientation.

Social orientation as a theme of importance is revealed in a response such as "The boy is waiting for the gang to come over" (Card II).

Additions: Where a characteristic is included in the theme despite the lack of a direct stimulus (such as music in the fireside scene), it is indicated by the appropriate abbreviation. If the characteristic is also part of the main theme, it is indicated in both "importance" and "additions;" if it is mentioned first, it is indicated in all three; "primacy," "importance," and "additions."

Unnoted: A part of the scene that is presented but not included in the story nor mentioned, such as the skis in the fireside scene or the radio in the scene with the boy, is noted here with a minus sign in front of it.

To obtain the total score, count "primacy" as 1 point, "importance" with exclamation as 2 points, without as 1 point. Do not count a casual mentioning unless it occurs twice, and then count it as 1 point. "Additions" count 1 point, and "unnoted" counts as minus 1 point. Collect a total score for each of the five orientations and mark it in the space at the bottom of the page.

RESPONSE FREQUENCY TABULATION AND RELATION BETWEEN PROJECTIVE AND EMPIRICAL TEST

The first part of this exercise consists of tabulating the response frequencies to various aspects of the pictures in the PIT. Each person in class should select one test at random. On Card 1, as the instructor mentions an item appearing on that card, indicate whether your subject mentioned that item anywhere in the report by raising your hand. Record these frequencies in Tables 12.1–12.3.

After the tabulation is completed, you will note that some items are seen and mentioned by most of the individuals in the group; others are rarely noticed. Even with a projective test, where we have a theory about what a response means, it is clear that we must have some normative data about responses. If everyone mentions the fire in Card 1, then the fire probably does not indicate much in the way of orientation unless it is not noted.

The reliability of the test and the level of agreement between scorers should be checked first. For purposes of this exercise, we will assume adequate test and scorer reliability.

The second part of the exercise is a validation of the projective test. Simply because there is a theory that suggests what a response ought to mean does not mean that a test is valid. A projective test can be validated in many ways. One way would be to check the interpretations to see if they will accurately predict the subjects' behavior. Another is to determine whether different criterion groups score differently on the test. In this case, we will relate the projective test score to another test that has been previously validated (criterion validity, concurrent).

We will demonstrate this type of validation by relating the PIT to the POT to see if they are measuring the same things. Each student should select one pair of tests given to the same subject (*not* one of the subjects used in the original criterion groups for the POT). Scores for 20 subjects from the two tests on the same scales ("gaming," etc.) should be recorded in Tables 12.4–12.8 and the correlation between the scores computed.

A high correlation between the two measures of the same trait indicates convergent validity. *Convergent validity* is evidence that two independently developed measurement methods "converge" on the same psychological variable. A high correlation between the two measures provides partial support for each of them.

Table 12.1 Card I–Living Room
Total N =

Item	Frequency	% Occurrence
Skis		
Table		
Coffee cups		
Ash tray		
Fireplace		
Fire		
Wine bottle		
Pillow		
Painting		
Candlestick		
Rug		
Floor		
Brick wall		
Plant		
Recipe box		
Kitchen		

Table 12.2 Card II–Boy Reading
Total N =

Item	Frequency	% Occurrence
Boy		
Book		
Glasses		
Radio		
Fruit		
Plate		
Table		
Lamp cord		
Bag chair		
Running shoes		
Ball		
Glove		
Tennis racket		
Checkerboard		

Table 12.3 Card III–People at Desk
Total N =

Item	Frequency	% Occurrence
Man		
Woman		
Radio		
Tape recorder		
Cassette tapes		
Books		
Notebooks		
Papers		
Pens		
Coffee cups		
Pop cans		
Fruit		
Candy bars		
Pack		
Ring		
Watch		
Calendar		

Table 12.4 Convergent Validity of PIT and POT: Gaming Scale

Subject	Picture Description Test Raw Score	Personal Orientation Test Raw Score	Picture Description Test Rank	Personal Orientation Test Rank	d	d²
A						
B						
C						
D						
E						
F						
G						
H						
I						
J						
K						
L						
M						
N						
O						
P						
Q						
R						
S						
T						

$$\text{rho} = 1.00 - \left(\frac{6\Sigma d^2}{N^3 - N} \right)$$

Table 12.5 Convergent Validity of PIT and POT: Sporting Scale

Subject	Picture Description Test Raw Score	Personal Orientation Test Raw Score	Picture Description Test Rank	Personal Orientation Test Rank	d	d²
A						
B						
C						
D						
E						
F						
G						
H						
I						
J						
K						
L						
M						
N						
O						
P						
Q						
R						
S						
T						

$$\text{rho} = 1.00 - \left(\frac{6\Sigma d^2}{N^3 - N} \right)$$

Table 12.6 Convergent Validity of PIT and POT: Gourmet Scale

Subject	Picture Description Test Raw Score	Personal Orientation Test Raw Score	Picture Description Test Rank	Personal Orientation Test Rank	d	d²
A						
B						
C						
D						
E						
F						
G						
H						
I						
J						
K						
L						
M						
N						
O						
P						
Q						
R						
S						
T						

$$\text{rho} = 1.00 - \left(\frac{6\Sigma d^2}{N^3 - N} \right)$$

Table 12.7 Convergent Validity of PIT and POT: Aesthetic Scale

Subject	Picture Description Test Raw Score	Personal Orientation Test Raw Score	Picture Description Test Rank	Personal Orientation Test Rank	d	d^2
A						
B						
C						
D						
E						
F						
G						
H						
I						
J						
K						
L						
M						
N						
O						
P						
Q						
R						
S						
T						

$$\text{rho} = 1.00 - \left(\frac{6\Sigma d^2}{N^3 - N} \right)$$

Table 12.8 Convergent Validity of PIT and POT: Social Scale

Subject	Picture Description Test Raw Score	Personal Orientation Test Raw Score	Picture Description Test Rank	Personal Orientation Test Rank	d	d^2
A						
B						
C						
D						
E						
F						
G						
H						
I						
J						
K						
L						
M						
N						
O						
P						
Q						
R						
S						
T						

$$\text{rho} = 1.00 - \left(\frac{6\Sigma d^2}{N^3 - N} \right)$$

Assignment for **EXERCISE 12**

1. Administer and score the PIT for three people. One subject should be a person who has already taken the POT.
2. Participate in the tabulation of responses.
3. Write up interpretations of the results for individuals you tested.
4. Answer the following questions:
   a. What difficulties, if any, did you have administering the PIT? What influence, if any, do you think *you* had on the examinees' responses?

   b. What are the relative advantages of the POT ("objective" questionnaire) and the PIT?

   c. Explain the rationale of a "projective" device and how this rationale applies to the PIT.

LABORATORY EXERCISE 13

Situational Testing: Leaderless Group Discussion

PURPOSE

The purpose of this exercise is to illustrate one type of situational test, the leaderless group discussion. In the exercise, the class will practice behavioral observation, behavioral recording, and the use of rating scales.

BACKGROUND

Paper and pencil tests measure only a relatively narrow range of cognitive and affective behavior. The typical aptitude, ability, or personality test measures characteristics which are specifically defined. They may be thought of as measures of relatively "molecular" behavior. In contrast, most situational tests call for more molar or global behaviors such as personal interaction or complex decision making. Sometimes called *performance tests,* these procedures usually require the examinee to talk with other people, solve complex problems, or even manipulate apparatus or equipment. Often, situational tests are simulations of important aspects of a task or job.

In many cases, an observer must watch the examinee in the situation exercise and record the behavior taking place or rate the examinee on rating scales. The observer plays a crucial role in the measurement process. The observer must be skilled at noting relevant behavior, objective in interpreting the behavior, and knowledgeable about the rating scales. The rating scales themselves must be developed well, and one process for doing so is included in Exercise 14.

PROCEDURE

The instructor will choose four students to be participants in the leaderless group discussion. These students will be given their instructions and sent to another room to prepare for the discussion. While they are gone, the instructor will arrange the room with a table and four chairs at the front so that the class can observe. Each remaining class member will be an observer and rater. The instructor should assign one-fourth of the class to observe each of the four participants.

INSTRUCTIONS TO OBSERVERS

While the participants are preparing for the discussion, the remainder of the class should prepare to observe. Form 13.1 should be used to take notes. Form 13.2 will be used to summarize the observations under dimensions and to rate performance on those dimensions.

To prepare for the observation, the class should:

1. Discuss the need to record *specific* behaviors displayed in the discussion.
2. Read and discuss the dimensions and their definitions.
3. Discuss the rating scale and the reference group to be used for comparison.

OBSERVATIONS

During the discussion, the class should take careful notes on Form 13.1. Form 13.2 should be completed as soon as possible after the discussion. Do not discuss the ratings with other students until the next laboratory session.

SUGGESTED READINGS

Anastasi, A. *Psychological Testing* (4th ed.). New York: Macmillan, 1976, pp. 593–598.

Brown, F. G. *Principles of Educational and Psychological Testing* (2nd ed.). New York: Holt, Rinehart and Winston, 1976, pp. 401–406.

Cronbach, L. J. *Essentials of Psychological Testing* (3rd ed.). New York: Harper & Row, 1970, pp. 646–649, 675–678.

Thorndike, R.L., and Hagan, E. *Measurement and Evaluation in Psychology and Education* (4th ed.). New York: Wiley, 1977, pp. 501–506.

INSTRUCTIONS TO PARTICIPANTS

You are one of a committee who have been selected from the student body by the dean of the college. The dean must make some important decisions and would like student opinions on these matters. Your committee is to provide this input to the dean. As a member of the committee, you should present your own ideas, and you also should strive to represent a broad sample of ideas from other students.

The committee's task is to provide *specific written* recommendations on each of the four problems described below. The recommendations should be a *consensus* of the entire committee. Each of you must sign the final recommendations to be submitted to the dean. You have____minutes for your discussion.

1. A professor has recently flunked a student for plagiarizing. The professor indicated that significant portions of a term paper were rephrased from another student's paper the previous year. The student has appealed the grade to the dean. How should the dean proceed?
2. At the end of the year, there are some unexpended funds. The dean intends to use $2000 on a project to increase the students' awareness of realistic career options. The committee is asked to recommend one specific project where this money should be spent.
3. It has been brought to the attention of the dean that a particular professor is an "easy grader." Complaints have come from both faculty and students (many from other sections of the same course) that the professor gives all A's. The course is a lecture-discussion class taken mainly by students in their sophomore and junior year. What action, if any, does the committee feel the dean should take?
4. The dean would like a list (in rank order of importance) of the three most pressing student concerns about the educational process at this campus. The dean will cite these concerns in a presentation to a potential funding agency.

Form 13.1 Observation Form

On this form, record specific observations you make about the person you are observing in the discussion. Write specific things the person says or does which reveal performance on the dimensions you will rate. On the right-hand side, write down brief comments by other participants so that you will know the context of your participant's comments.

Behavioral Observations for _____	*Observations for Other Participants*

Form 13.1 Observation Form

On this form, record specific observations you make about the person you are observing in the discussion. Write specific things the person says or does which reveal performance on the dimensions you will rate. On the right-hand side, write down brief comments by other participants so that you will know the context of your participant's comments.

Behavioral Observations for _____	*Observations for Other Participants*

Form 13.2 Observation Summary and Ratings

On this form, write examples of behavior which illustrate the person's performance on each dimension. Include positive and negative examples. After all observations are categorized, rate the person's performance on each dimension using the scale: 1—very poor, 2—below average, 3—average, 4—above average, 5—excellent.

Dimension   **Rating**

Oral Communication   1 2 3 4 5

Speaking clearly and concisely, using nonverbal communication, listening well.

Energy   1 2 3 4 5

Maintaining a high level of interest and activity in the discussion.

Leadership   1 2 3 4 5

Effectiveness in guiding a group to accomplish a task, including contributing good ideas and managing the group's time.

Problem Solving   1 2 3 4 5

Effectiveness in seeking out pertinent data, determining source of a problem, suggesting possible solutions, and making a good choice.

Empathy   1 2 3 4 5

Skill in perceiving accurately the thoughts and feelings of other people including individuals in the cases and other participants.

Form 13.2 Observation Summary and Ratings

On this form, write examples of behavior which illustrate the person's performance on each dimension. Include positive and negative examples. After all observations are categorized, rate the person's performance on each dimension using the scale: 1—very poor, 2—below average, 3—average, 4—above average, 5—excellent.

Dimension   **Rating**

Oral Communication   1   2   3   4   5

    Speaking clearly and concisely, using nonverbal communication, listening well.

Energy   1   2   3   4   5

    Maintaining a high level of interest and activity in the discussion.

Leadership   1   2   3   4   5

    Effectiveness in guiding a group to accomplish a task, including contributing good ideas and managing the group's time.

Problem Solving   1   2   3   4   5

    Effectiveness in seeking out pertinent data, determining source of a problem, suggesting possible solutions, and making a good choice.

Empathy   1   2   3   4   5

    Skill in perceiving accurately the thoughts and feelings of other people including individuals in the cases and other participants.

Assignment for **EXERCISE 13**

1. Observe the discussion and complete Forms 13.1 and 13.2 for one participant.
2. Write a summary of the participant's role in the discussion and your assessment of the participant's strengths and weaknesses in the dimensions you observed.
3. Answer the following questions:
    a. Briefly describe two advantages of situational tests, for example, the leaderless group discussion, in comparison with paper and pencil tests.

    b. List four characteristics of good behavioral observations (e.g., the observations should be *specific* rather than general).

    c. What errors of measurement might affect the ratings given in this exercise?

LABORATORY EXERCISE 14

Behaviorally Anchored Rating Scales

PURPOSE

This exercise is designed to give the student experience in the construction of rating scales using the retranslation of behavior procedure. This procedure results in a Behaviorally Anchored Rating (BAR) scale. BAR scales have been developed to overcome many of the biases or errors which affect ratings, namely, leniency, halo, central tendency, and low interjudge reliability. In industrial settings, BAR scales are used as a measure of performance effectiveness for employees. In school settings, they have been used for rating teacher and student effectiveness.

BAR SCALES

In general, the BAR scale is a rating format with both numbers and behavior examples. The numbers range from 1 to 5, 1 to 7, or 1 to 9. The illustrative examples of behavior are used as anchors to help the rater define specific points on the scale. Rating scales assess more than one dimension (area) of performance. There would be a separate BAR scale, with different anchors, for each dimension. For example, a BAR scale for "student performance" might include the dimension "class participation." The final BAR scale for this dimension might look like:

Class participation: The student's willingness to ask and answer questions, and share relevant ideas with the class.

9 ―

8 ― ← This student makes contributions showing insight and integration of concepts.

7 ―

6 ― ← This student asks questions relevant to the topic at hand.

5 ―

4 ― ← This student attempts to answer questions but does not volunteer anything to a discussion.

3 ―

2 ― ← This student sleeps through most class sessions.

1 ― ← This student does not attend class except for tests.

Rating_____

239

As can be seen from this example, the behavior examples are anchored to the scale by arrows, and the dimension title and definition are included for the rater. The development of a BAR scale involves people familiar with the performance area to be analyzed. Different groups of participants are used throughout the process enabling the developers to only include dimensions and anchors where there is a great deal of agreement between the participants.

BAR PROCEDURE

There are six basic steps for developing BAR scales.

Step 1. Individuals familiar with the job, position, or area being assessed are asked to generate *critical incidents*. These critical incidents are examples of effective and ineffective performance related to the area. A list of 300 examples is not unrealistic. Participants included in this step can be supervisors, people in the position, subordinates, or trained observers.

Step 2. The test developers cluster these critical incidents into performance dimensions. This clustering is an inferential process by the developers using their knowledge and feel for the job. Each dimension is given a short title and a one-sentence definition.

Step 3. The next step is to retranslate the behaviors. A second group of participants is given the list of statements and the list of dimensions, but they are not informed of the prior categorization of behaviors. Participants are asked to assign each behavioral illustration to a dimension. Upon completion of these judgments by the participants, the developers retain only those statements where there is large agreement as to which dimension the statement belongs. Test developers use a criterion of between 60–80 percent agreement.

Step 4. Retained items (those of high agreement) are then grouped according to dimension, and a third group of participants is asked to rate numerically each item (on say a 9-point scale) of low to high effectiveness. Items are retained at this stage only if there is high agreement as to scale value. On a 9-point scale, a standard deviation of 1.0 or less would indicate sufficient agreement.

Step 5. Dimensions themselves are now analyzed by the developers. Each retained statement is placed at its mean scale value on its dimension. To be used as a BAR scale, a dimension must not have large "gaps" where there are no behavioral examples as anchors. On a 9-point scale, the developer may consider a scale interval of three units as too large. Any dimensions that have gaps larger than three scale units are deleted from the final rating scales. Of course, this means that all the behavior examples from that dimension are deleted also. To keep the dimension from being too overloaded with anchors, only about six to eight items are retained on a 9-point BAR scale.

Step 6. The final scales are prepared. The dimension title and definition are placed at the top to aid the rater in understanding the area being assessed. Each anchor has an arrow or line drawn to its mean scale value, as determined in Step 4. A place for a numeric rating may be included for ease of scoring. Additionally, space can be left at the bottom of the scale for comments by the raters. Some raters feel "shorted" when they cannot explain their ratings. Comments can add understanding to a person's performance evaluation. More importantly to the test developer, comments on the rating scale itself are an important source of feedback for continually reevaluating the scale's impact on the rater.

ADVANTAGES OF BAR SCALES

BAR scales are widely used because of the many advantages offered. The rating form is based on job related activities which increases "face validity." The rating scale includes a definition of the dimension. Scale points are defined by behaviors, not just numbers. The behavior anchors are written by persons connected with the job and familiar with the terminology of the job being assessed. There can be more credibility in the ratings because of the personal involvement in the development by job members. The feedback to the person being assessed can be clearer as it points to examples of behavior. Proponents of BAR scales argue that they result in increased reliability, less halo, and fewer response biases in ratings.

DISADVANTAGES OF BAR SCALES

There are some difficulties with the BAR. A very large number of participants are needed in the development if each step is to have a different group participating. It is a very time-consuming process. Retranslation of 500 items takes about two hours. It becomes expensive to use hundreds of hours when large numbers of managers participate.

EXPECTATION TERMINOLOGY

The behavioral illustrations given for the rating scales used in this exercise deal with teacher evaluation. They are written in expectation terminology. Instead of saying, "Examinations are challenging," it says, "Examinations could be expected to be challenging." After Step 2, the test developers change the wording of "the critical incidents" to contain the word "expected." Step 3, then, becomes "retranslation of expectations" instead of "retranslation of behaviors." Expectation terminology is not a requirement. Its advantage lies in the fact that the actual behavior did not have to be observed but only inferred. The important drawback is that expectation terminology becomes very repetitive and irritating to participants and raters.

LABORATORY PROCEDURES FOR THIS EXERCISE

1. This is an exercise in developing BAR scales for assessing teacher effectiveness. Step 1, generating critical incidents, has been completed and resulted in 50 behavioral examples. Step 2, inferring dimensions, has also been completed and resulted in 10 dimensions. Your class should discuss the meaning of these dimensions and clarify their meaning in your school. You are to be the participants in Step 3, the retranslation process. Using the instructions in Form 14.1 and the dimension titles and definitions in Form 14.2, assign each of the 50 behavioral examples in Form 14.3 to a dimension.
2. Using the tally sheet in Table 14.1, record the results of your class. Starting with Item 1, put a tally mark for each person who classified the behavior in each dimension. Do this for all 50 items. Calculate 65 percent of your class size. For each item, circle the tally marks if they exceed that 65 percent. For items with 65 percent or less agreement in all dimensions, draw an "X" through the item number. Items with an "X" would be dropped from further analysis. Items without an "X" would be assigned to the dimension in the column of the circle.
3. Refer to Table 14.2. These are data from a sample of 35 other students. In this case, an item must have 23 respondents to be retained. Use the same procedure for analysis as in number 2 above. Compare your class results with those of the exercise sample. (*Note*: At this point, your instructor will indicate whether you use your class data or data from Table 14.2.)
4. Retained items would now be scaled. The items would be grouped by dimension and given to a set of judges, who may be the students in your class or some other students. The participants should assign each item within a dimension a number between 1 and 9 with 1 being "very low effectiveness" and 9 being "very high effectiveness." Table 14.3 consists of the means and standard deviation for each item after scaling by a new group of participants, with an N of 40. The rejection criterion for non-agreement of scale values was chosen to be 2.00. (In practice, you would have more items and could set a lower value.) Draw a line through any item that has a standard deviation of 2.00 or greater. These items would be deleted from further analysis.
5. Place the remaining items at the appropriate scale point of their respective dimensions in Form 14.4 (pages 253–267). The dimensions "organization" and "surroundings" have not been included as each had only one anchor. To select final scales, the criterion that there are no gaps larger than three units must be met. Place a large "X" across the scales that do not meet this criterion. The remaining scales are your final forms for teacher effectiveness ratings using the BAR scaling procedure and starting with the 50 given behavior examples. This is why it is very important to generate a large number of critical incidents in Step 1.

The instructions given to the raters, using a BAR scale, are shown in Form 14.5. Instructions are very important. No matter how well you have developed your rating scales, the data gathered are meaningless if the raters do not understand the rating method. Form 14.5 should be used to introduce the rating scales to a student who will rate one professor.

SUGGESTED READINGS

Anastasi, A. *Psychological Testing* (4th ed.). New York: Macmillan, 1976, pp. 609–611.
Cronbach, L. J. *Essentials of Psychological Testing* (3rd ed.). New York: Harper & Row, 1970, pp. 571–584.
Gronlund, N. E. *Measurement and Evaluation in Teaching* (3rd ed.). New York: Macmillan, 1976, pp. 435–445.

Mehrens, W. A., and Lehmann, I. J. *Measurement and Evaluation in Education and Psychology* (2nd ed.). New York: Holt, Rinehart and Winston, 1975, pp. 354–364.

Thorndike, R. L., and Hagan, E. *Measurement and Evaluation in Psychology and Education* (4th ed.). New York: Wiley, 1977, pp. 448–466.

Form 14.1   Instructions

This experiment deals with college teaching. Traditional methods of evaluating teaching leave a lot to be desired; for example, they do not point out specific weaknesses to the person being evaluated so that appropriate changes in behavior can be made. Research seems to indicate that these problems can be overcome by using rating scales that focus on the behavior of teachers. As part of the development of this procedure, a number of behavioral examples have been collected from other students. What we are trying to do now is to see if these behaviors have something in common. We would like for you to give us your opinion about which of the 10 dimensions described on the following page best characterizes each of these behaviors. Let's try a few examples. First, tear out the reference sheet containing the list of dimensions (Form 14.2), and study their definitions. When you have completed that, we will go over the following examples.

EXAMPLE 1

1. Dimension_____Questions on examinations could be expected to be clearly stated and representative of material covered in the course; tests are learning experiences.
   Checking the reference sheet, this seems to be an example of testing; so a "T" is entered as the dimension.

EXAMPLE 2

2. Dimension_____The professor could be expected to rely heavily on notes and frequently be unable to answer questions from students.
   If, after checking the reference sheet, you felt this was an example of the competence dimension, you would write a "C" after "Dimension."

Note: We are interested in your personal evaluations of these items, and it is important for you to fill in each item, even though some may be ambiguous.

Form 14.2   Performance Dimensions of Teaching Behavior

Note: Only one dimension may be assigned to each item.

C. *Competence:* Professor is thoroughly competent in subject being studied.

D. *Delivery:* The way course content is conveyed to students.

E. *Enthusiasm:* Excitement about subject matter is generated by the professor, which stimulates thought.

F. *Faculty-student interaction:* Faculty-student relationships are cooperative, and the interpersonal environment is conducive to learning.

G. *Goals and objectives:* Course objectives are defined at the onset and followed throughout the course; an overview of the course is presented.

I. *Integration:* Course topics flow logically to provide a cohesive whole.

M. *Methods:* Use of media sources (slides, videotapes, etc.) involving all the senses.

O. *Organization:* The extent to which the course content is arranged in a systematic and balanced fashion; the appropriate allocation of time to topics within the course, and the timely availability of course materials.

S. *Surrounding:* Utilization of environmental factors to facilitate learning and alleviate boredom.

T. *Testing:* Evaluating procedures are consistent with course objectives, require thought more than memorization, and can be viewed as learning experiences.

Form 14.3   Behavioral Examples to Be Classified

 1. Dimension_____It could be expected that only part of the available media sources would be used.
 2. Dimension_____The instructor could be expected to show little confidence in himself or herself and the subject matter that is being taught.
 3. Dimension_____This instructor could be expected to answer any questions about the material and to display an aura of confidence.
 4. Dimension_____This professor could be expected to speak too fast or be repetitious.
 5. Dimension_____The course could be expected to provide case histories which would facilitate understanding and provide a means of testing myself to see if I know it or not.
 6. Dimension_____It could be expected that the students would have to walk clear across campus to attend class in a classroom with poor acoustics, but which just happens to be across the hall from the instructor's office.
 7. Dimension_____This professor could be expected to be easily approachable on some occasions and difficult to approach on others.
 8. Dimension_____Examinations could be expected to be challenging.
 9. Dimension_____This professor could be expected to be familiar with current articles, to offer ideas spontaneously, and to present rational arguments for a case.
10. Dimension_____The professor could be expected to be willing to work with students.
11. Dimension_____The course could be expected to make me think and to allow for questions and answers during the lecture.
12. Dimension_____This course could be expected to have topics arranged in a logical order but to not have them tied together very well.
13. Dimension_____This professor could be expected to be difficult to find and to not care if the students understand the material.
14. Dimension_____This instructor could be expected to spend a lot of time answering involved questions from the smarter students.
15. Dimension_____The course could be expected to be well organized, emphasizing important information and eliminating superfluous details.
16. Dimension_____This professor's interest and enthusiasm could be expected to stimulate the students to do some reading they would not have done on their own.
17. Dimension_____This professor could be expected to define course objectives and to not deviate from them during the semester.
18. Dimension_____The professor could be expected to establish a congenial attitude with the class.
19. Dimension_____It could be expected that all the things discussed in the course seem to fit together, and each part would make everything else more interesting.
20. Dimension_____The professor's complete lack of interest in the subject could be expected to turn the students off to the subject.
21. Dimension_____This professor could not be expected to handle classroom situations correctly on a day-to-day basis.
22. Dimension_____If necessary, the course could be expected to provide illustrative examples.
23. Dimension_____Examinations could be expected to be inconsistent in terms of difficulty (i.e., some exam questions would be fair and thought-provoking while others would be too easily answered, too unclear, or would not be related to the immediate course objectives).
24. Dimension_____If the particular class were of more than an hour's duration, it would be expected that a break would be provided the students so as to preclude lapse of attention.

25. Dimension_____The professor could be expected to fail to generate any excitement in lecture presentations.
26. Dimension_____Believing that her or his ideas and philosophies are the only right ones, this professor could not be expected to listen to the students' points of view.
27. Dimension_____This professor could be expected to have had practical experience and can speak 'off the cuff' about important issues in the field.
28. Dimension_____This professor could be expected to fail to challenge the students to look, read, and study more in an effort to gain additional knowledge.
29. Dimension_____It could be expected that the material would be presented only by lecture and that no alternative sources would be utilized.
30. Dimension_____This professor could be expected to have little knowledge of the subject and to be unable to apply what is known.
31. Dimension_____This professor could be expected to sometimes rush through important material, while stressing that which is not as important.
32. Dimension_____At times, this professor could be expected to be inadequately prepared to explain the material or to answer questions.
33. Dimension_____It could be expected that the room and surrounding environment would actually hinder learning.
34. Dimension_____Exams could be expected to have clearly stated objective questions with clear, non-ambiguous choices as responses.
35. Dimension_____This professor could be expected to define goals for a course that are reasonable, realistic, and well thought out.
36. Dimension_____This professor could be expected to use poor English and be nearly impossible to understand.
37. Dimension_____Examinations in this class could be expected to require regurgitation of meaningless facts.
38. Dimension_____This professor could be expected to use correct English, to pronounce words well, and to speak at a comfortable pace.
39. Dimension_____The tests could be expected to see how well you could memorize and not to make you think and relate course material to real-life situations.
40. Dimension_____This professor could be expected to leave the students the task of defining the course objectives or to define them in such broad terms (i.e., know everything) that the objectives are meaningless.
41. Dimension_____This course could be expected to flow in a logical pattern.
42. Dimension_____This course could not be expected to fulfill its objectives given at the onset of the semester.
43. Dimension_____This course could be expected to have irrelevant, poorly stated objectives.
44. Dimension_____Exams in this course could be expected to stimulate thinking and accurately evaluate one's ability to make the material practical.
45. Dimension_____This course could be expected to emphasize details only, with no overall picture given.
46. Dimension_____This professor could be expected to cover the material in a natural progression with just enough time to properly cover each lecture.
47. Dimension_____This professor could be expected to be compulsively late and to present very unstructured lectures.
48. Dimension_____Course material could be expected to be completely out of any rational sequence.
49. Dimension_____It could be expected that the students would have to extend some attention to being comfortable or to seeing.
50. Dimension_____This professor could be expected to use "sick" or "off-color" jokes when giving lectures.

Table 14.1 Tally Sheet for Retranslation of Behaviors

Item #	Dimension									
	C	D	E	F	G	I	M	O	S	T
1										
2										
3										
4										
5										
6										
7										
8										
9										
10										
11										
12										
13										
14										
15										
16										
17										
18										
19										
20										
21										
22										
23										
24										

Table 14.1 (*Continued*)

Dimension

Item #	C	D	E	F	G	I	M	O	S	T
25										
26										
27										
28										
29										
30										
31										
32										
33										
34										
35										
36										
37										
38										
39										
40										
41										
42										
43										
44										
45										
46										
47										
48										
49										
50										

Table 14.2 Step 3: Retranslation of Behavior — Results of Assigning Critical Incidents to Dimensions

Dimension

Item #	C	D	E	F	G	I	M	O	S	T
1	1	1					30	2	1	
2	27	6	1		1					
3	30			1	2		1	1		
4	1	31		1			1	1		
5	2	4	1		1		9	6	5	7
6		1	1	4				1	28	
7	2		1	31					1	
8	2	1						1		31
9	27	4	3						1	
10	2		2	31						
11	1	11	4	12	1	1		5		
12		1	1		1	23		8		1
13	1	1	4	29						
14	3			30		1		1		
15	1	5				1		28		
16	1		34							
17		1			30	1		2		1
18	1		5	28		1				
19					1	27		6		1
20	3		31							1
21	19	1		8		1		5	1	
22		3	2		2	25		1	2	
23		1						1		33
24	4	10	3	1			2	13		
25		4	29	1					1	

Dimension

Item #	C	D	E	F	G	I	M	O	S	T
26	3	3	2	27						
27	28	4	3							
28	4		21	6				1		3
29		5				23	1	6		
30	31	3			1					
31	3	22	1		2	2		5		
32	26	2						7		
33		1							34	
34					1					34
35	2	2	1		29	1				
36	3	31							1	
37			1		1			1		32
38	3	31						1		
39					1		1		1	32
40	3	4	1		23	1	1	1		1
41				1	29			3		2
42	1	1	1		28	1		3		
43		1			30	2		1		1
44	1									34
45	1	10			14	4		6		
46		5		1		7	1	21		
47	6	7	3			1		18		
48		2			2	16		14		1
49		1							34	
50		29	1	1		1		1	2	

Table 14.3 Step 4: Results After Scaling Each Item Within Its Dimension[a]

Dimension	Item #	$\bar{X}$	SD	Dimension	Item #	$\bar{X}$	SD
C	2	2.450	1.947	G	17	7.150	1.562
C	3	8.425	1.083	G	35	8.675	0.656
C	9	8.600	0.871	G	40	2.100	1.429
C	27	6.175	1.866	G	42	3.100	2.205
C	30	1.675	1.509	G	43	1.400	0.810
C	32	3.675	1.992	I	12	5.225	1.609
D	4	3.375	1.957	I	19	8.550	0.783
D	36	1.450	1.319	I	41	8.150	1.027
D	38	8.025	1.544	M	1	5;075	1.730
D	50	2.875	1.786	M	22	7.900	1.392
E	16	8.600	1.057	M	29	3.255	1.957
E	20	1.675	1.366	O	15	7.975	1.459
E	25	2.100	1.317	S	6	2.650	1.961
F	7	4.769	1.358	S	33	2.375	2.059
F	10	8.667	0.772	S	49	4.425	2.531
F	13	1.436	0.995	T	8	6.525	1.853
F	14	3.769	2.071	T	23	4.800	1.786
F	18	6.641	1.347	T	34	8.450	1.145
F	26	2.103	1.832	T	37	2.050	1.616
				T	39	3.300	2.210
				T	44	6.950	1.239

[a]Scaled: 1—very low effectiveness—to 9—very high effectiveness.

Note: This table includes only 40 items, as 10 items failed to meet the retranslation criterion in Step 3.

Form 14.4

Competence: Professor is thoroughly competent in subject being studied.

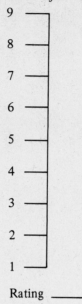

Rating _____

Delivery: The way course content is conveyed to students.

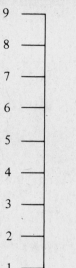

Rating _____

Faculty-student interaction: Faculty-student relationships are cooperative, and the interpersonal environment is conducive to learning.

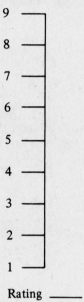

Rating _____

Enthusiasm: Excitement about subject matter is generated by the professors, which stimulates thought.

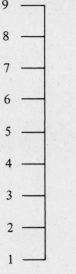

Rating _____

Goals and objectives: Course objectives are defined at the onset and followed throughout the course; an overview of the course is presented.

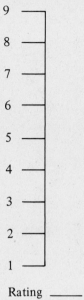

Rating _____

Integration: Course topics flow logically to provide a cohesive whole.

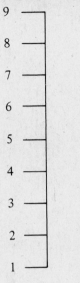

Rating _____

Methods: Use of media sources (slides, videotapes, etc.) involving all the senses.

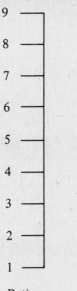

Rating _____

Testing: Evaluation procedures are consistent with course objectives, require more than memorization, and can be viewed as learning experiences.

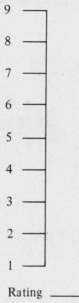

Rating _____

_Name _____

Form 14.5   Course and Instructor Evaluation

INSTRUCTIONS:

On the following _____ pages are _____ dimensions which are critical elements in the evaluation of a course and its instructor. Each page lists one dimension, the definition of that dimension, and a scale ranging from 1 (low) to 9 (high) for rating the course and instructor on that dimension. At various levels of the scale are behavioral illustrations of the dimension which you will find helpful in understanding the dimension.

THE TASK:

Your task is to rate your course or instructor on each of the _____ dimensions by placing a slash (/) at the point on each scale which most accurately reflects your own feelings about this course or instructor. In addition to actually "slashing" a scale, please copy your numerical rating in the space provided at the bottom of the scale. You should feel free to use numbers other than whole numbers. For example, you may rate your instructor on teaching methods as 3, 3.1, or 3.15.

PLEASE MAKE COMMENTS!!

Space is provided below each scale for you to make specific comments about the course or instructor as they relate to the particular dimension under consideration. Please be sure your comment reflects the rating you have given. These are *most* important to the evaluation effort and will be summarized and provided as feedback to the instructor.

   Thank you for your cooperation!

Assignment for **EXERCISE 14**

1. Complete the analysis requested by your instructor.
2. Prepare the final rating scales for the dimensions which "survived" the procedure. Show the behavioral anchors for several points on the rating scale.
3. Use the scale by observing and rating a professor in a class.
4. Answer the following questions:
   a. What are the advantages of the BARS?

   b. What is the "retranslation" phase of the process?

   c. Why do you think it was (and usually is) difficult to find anchors for the middle of BARS?

LABORATORY EXERCISE 15
Criterion-Referenced Testing

PURPOSE

This exercise illustrates how criterion-referenced tests differ from the more familiar norm-referenced tests, and how these differences affect the test construction and test evaluation processes.

CRITERION-REFERENCED TESTS

Criterion-referenced tests differ from norm-referenced tests because they are designed for a different purpose. Whereas a norm-referenced test compares each individual to other individuals who take the test by using such statistics as percentiles, a criterion-referenced test compares individuals to a criterion (hence, the name "criterion referenced"). A criterion-referenced test is interpreted in terms of whether or not the individual meets some standard level of performance in a specifically defined domain of behavior. Criterion-referenced testing should not be confused with criterion related validity which refers to a correlation between test scores and a performance measure.

Criterion-referenced tests are appropriate in situations where the content area can be defined quite specifically and can be adequately represented by test items, where there is some fairly logical sequence of knowledge or skills to be acquired, and where there is no limitation on how many examinees can pass. Examples include mathematics courses, driver licensing, or certification of plumbers. It is often desirable for everyone who takes the test to get all the items correct. For example, after a unit of training is completed, the educator might hope to certify all the students as competent in the area of the training.

However, there are certain performance domains for which criterion-referenced testing is inappropriate. These include such advanced and less structured courses as law and physics. In such subjects, individuals may progress in understanding and originality by acquiring different patterns of knowledge and may advance virtually without limit. Moreover, content coverage is made even more difficult in that learning may extend in many directions or specialties.

TEST WRITING AND ITEM ANALYSIS

Since the criterion-referenced test is specifically linked to a performance domain, it is important that all aspects of the domain be adequately covered by the test items. (This is also true of norm-referenced tests.) A valuable aid to help in ensuring adequate coverage is a test plan which specifies the aspects of the topic to be measured and the weight of each aspect in terms of the number of items used to measure it. A process similar to this was carried out in Exercise 6 when developing the Psychological Achievement Test.

Even though test items have been carefully constructed in accordance with a test plan, they should be analyzed to ensure that they function properly. Since the function of items in a criterion-referenced test is to discriminate between those who have mastered a subject area and those who have not, items are evaluated by giving them to two groups—one of which has been identified through its performance as having mastered the subject area, and another group which is similar to the mastery group in all respects except that it is composed of individuals who are nonmasters of the subject area. Items are chosen to maximize discrimination between the two groups but still adequately cover areas specified in the test plan.

VALIDITY AND RELIABILITY

Here again, criterion-referenced tests are different. The meaning of a norm-referenced test score depends on the relative position of the score in comparison with other scores. The more variability in test scores the better, because variability helps to distinguish between individuals. In contrast, variability is irrelevant in criterion-referenced test scores because their meaning comes directly from the connection between test content and the performance domain. It is, of course, true that scores on psychological tests always vary somewhat; however, variability is not a necessary condition for a good criterion-referenced test.

A major assumption involved when computing correlation coefficients is that there is range or variability in the numbers being correlated. Since criterion-referenced test scores may not vary (i.e., all individuals can get high scores), correlation coefficients may not be informative about reliability and validity. Restriction in range of scores will yield artificially low estimates of reliability and validity and, therefore, other measures are needed. A number of different validity and reliability measures have been proposed, but there is still not complete agreement about which ones are best. Since it is beyond the scope of this exercise to consider the relative merits of various methods of estimating validity and reliability for criterion-referenced tests, a simple measure of each will be presented with the understanding that the issue has yet to be resolved.

Validity can be assessed by determining how well the test assigns individuals who have been identified as masters or nonmasters to their proper groups. In the chart below, "a" indicates the masters who passed the test, and "d" indicates the nonmasters who failed the test.

Criterion Groups

		Masters	*Nonmasters*
Test Results	Pass	a	b
	Fail	c	d

An index of validity can be computed as follows:

$$\text{Validity} = \frac{\text{Number properly classified}}{\text{Total}} = \frac{a + d}{a + b + c + d}$$

This index of validity for a criterion-referenced test is simply the proportion of individuals who were properly classified by the test.

Although it will not be included in the procedure of this exercise, reliability can also be assessed with a proportional index. For example, the proportion of individuals who are classified the same way (either pass or fail) by parallel forms of the test can be calculated as an index of reliability.

MASTERY SCORES

The "mastery score" is the minimum level required to pass the test. Ideally the mastery score is based on a knowledge of what constitutes the required level of competence in the subject matter area being tested. However, our knowledge of what actually constitutes adequate performance is often inadequate; so other approaches may be necessary. One strategy is to choose a mastery score which maximizes validity as the proportion of individuals who are properly classified by the test. This has the advantage of setting the mastery score at the point which minimizes classification errors.

STEPS IN CONSTRUCTING
A CRITERION-REFERENCED TEST

1. Define *performance domain* in terms of specific behaviors or knowledge and level of competence expected of masters.
2. Construct a test plan which specifies the areas to be covered and the number of items needed for each area.
3. Write test items. Quite a few more items should be written than are needed so that poor items can be dropped and so that there will still be enough good items to cover all aspects of the performance domain.

4. Administer the items to two groups—one of which has been identified as masters in the criterion area, and one of which can be considered nonmasters. Care must be taken to ensure that the groups are as alike as possible in all respects except for their mastery of the criterion.
5. Select items which best discriminate between the master and nonmaster groups, and provide the number and types of items specified in the test plan.
6. Administer the test to other groups of masters and nonmasters and compute validity and reliability.

PROCEDURE FOR LAB

Steps 1–5

For the purposes of this exercise, assume that Steps 1–5 have already been carried out. The performance domain to be covered was knowledge and application of facts and principles in the following areas of automotive mechanics: engine repair, automatic transmission, manual transmission and rear axle, front end, brakes, electrical systems, engine functioning, engine tuneup, and fuel systems. Several items were written for each area. Some questions were borrowed from a sample test devised by the National Institute for Automotive Service Excellence; some were taken from previously prepared tests in academic courses in automotive mechanics; still others were specially written for this exercise.

The test was administered to two groups. One group was identified as the mastery group and included certified automotive mechanics. The other group was identified as the nonmastery group and included individuals not involved with automobile maintenance to any degree. Individuals in both groups were male and all were between the ages of 20 and 35.

From the original pool of items, 21 items were selected which best discriminated between the mastery and nonmastery groups, that is, those items which the mechanics tended to answer correctly and the nonmechanics tended to answer incorrectly. Moreover, items were deleted which the mechanics identified as either "tricky" or as having more than one possible answer. The number of items chosen for each test area were as follows:

Number of Items	Area	Questionnaire Numbers
2	Engine repair	14, 7
3	Automatic transmission	2, 12, 10
1	Manual transmission and rear axle	15
2	Front end	11, 17
3	Brakes	13, 21, 18
1	Electrical systems	19
3	Engine functioning	3, 5, 9
2	Engine tune-up	16, 20
4	Fuel systems	1, 4, 8, 6

Step 6. Administer the Test and Compute Validity

1. *Identification of criterion groups.* This step is very important since the basic purpose of the exercise is to validate a questionnaire which supposedly can distinguish between two separate groups of individuals. Thus, the student must be careful to correctly identify members of the two criterion groups. The definition of each criterion group is listed in Table 15.1. The class should discuss the characteristics of the two groups until the students have as clear a picture as possible of the individuals they will ask to participate.
2. *Administration of the test to the criterion groups.* Each student should locate two persons for each criterion group and administer the test to them. Keep in mind that it is not necessary for a masters person to be an actual certified automotive mechanic. However, each masters person should be matched with a nonmasters person of the same sex in order to avoid the possibility of obtaining a predominantly female pool of nonmasters individuals. If you have difficulty locating masters, go to a local service station or shop or ask your acquaintances to suggest someone. After administering each test, list your name as the examiner and by "code" write "master" or "nonmaster."
3. *Tabulation of responses for each group.* Each student should score his or her tests according to the answer key at the end of this exercise. A table identical to Table 15.2 should be drawn on the blackboard

allowing the subjects to be pooled and properly tallied. Students should record the final tally in their own workbooks.

4. *Compute validity*. The procedure for computing validity estimates is described on the assignment page.

SUGGESTED READINGS

Anastasi, A. *Psychological Testing* (4th ed.). New York: Macmillan, 1976, pp. 96–100, 131–133.

Brown, F. G. *Principles of Educational and Psychological Testing* (2nd ed.). New York: Holt, Rinehart and Winston, 1976, pp. 202–207, 246–248.

Cronbach, L. J. *Essentials of Psychological Testing* (3rd ed.). New York: Harper & Row, 1970, pp. 84–85.

Gronlund, N. E. *Measurement and Evaluation in Teaching* (3rd ed.). New York: Macmillan, 1976, pp. 18–20, 31–33, 142–143, 153–154, 271–274.

Mehrens, W. A., and Lehmann, I. J. *Measurement and Evaluation in Education and Psychology* (2nd ed.). New York: Holt, Rinehart and Winston, 1975, pp. 49–61, 106–107, 129–130, 178–179, 201–202, 333–334.

Thorndike, R. L., and Hagan, E. *Measurement and Evaluation in Psychology and Education* (4th ed.). New York: Wiley, 1977, pp. 5, 94–98, 166–176, 182–188.

Table 15.1 Description of Characteristics for the Criterion Groups

Masters: This person has an active interest in automotive mechanics, and spends many hours reading and discussing automotive mechanics. Moreover, this person maintains the proper functioning of an automobile: personally keeps the car in tune, takes apart and makes proper adjustments on parts, and buys and installs new parts if needed. This person is often asked for automotive advice and tips from other people. Ideally, this person should be a certified automotive mechanic.

Nonmasters: This person is not interested in automotive mechanics nor knowledgeable about the topic. The most maintenance provided to a car by this person includes checking the oil level, battery water level, and air pressure in the tires. The car is taken to a mechanic for all maintenance work including tune-ups, oil change, lubrication, and installation of new parts.

Table 15.2 Tally Sheet

Number Correct	Masters Group Tally	Number	Nonmasters Group Tally	Number
21				
20				
19				
18				
17				
16				
15				
14				
13				
12				
11				
10				
9				
8				
7				
6				
5				
4				
3				
2				
1				
0				

Assignment for **EXERCISE 15**

1. Administer the criterion-referenced test to two individuals identified as belonging to the masters group and to two individuals identified as belonging to the nonmasters group.
2. After the class has tallied the scores for all participants in Table 15.2, compute validity coefficients using the following formula:

$$\text{Validity} = \frac{a + d}{a + b + c + d}$$

where

a = number of masters people who passed
b = number of nonmasters people who passed
c = number of masters people who failed
d = number of nonmasters people who failed

a. Obtain validity coefficients using each of the following mastery scores: 15, 14, 13, 12, and 11. For example, if 14 is the mastery score, all individuals with scores of 14 or above would be considered as having passed the test.

When mastery score is 15, validity = _____
When mastery score is 14, validity = _____
When mastery score is 13, validity = _____
When mastery score is 12, validity = _____
When mastery score is 11, validity = _____

b. Which mastery score is best? Why?

3. Answer the following questions:
   a. What are the advantages of criterion-referenced testing over norm-referenced testing?

   b. What are the disadvantages of criterion-referenced testing versus norm-referenced testing?

c. List at least three specific subject-matter areas for which each of the above types of testing would be most suitable.

Criterion Reference	Norm Reference
1.	1.
2.	2.
3.	3.

d. Is it possible to make incorrect inferences or predictions from the results of an individual's criterion-referenced test results? Explain, using the automotive test in this exercise as an example.

Automotive Mechanics Test

Answer each of the following items by circling the correct answer. Answer every item. There is only one correct answer per item.

1. The circuit that controls the fuel level in the carburetor is the
   (a) Idle circuit
   (b) Float circuit
   (c) Power circuit
   (d) Choke circuit
2. A *stall test* can be used to check
   (a) Planetary gear noise
   (b) Governor pressure
   (c) Converter one-way clutch
   (d) Erratic shifting
3. The distributor shaft turns 360° for each time the engine rotates
   (a) 360°
   (b) 720°
   (c) 90°
   (d) 540°
4. Vapor lock is caused by
   (a) Using premium fuel
   (h) Too much heat on the fuel pump and lines
   (c) Too much fuel pump pressure
   (d) All the above
5. Which stroke of a four-cycle engine creates vacuum?
   (a) Intake
   (b) Exhaust
   (c) Compression
   (d) Power
6. Carburetor power circuits are *usually* brought into operation by
   (a) A decreasing fuel level in the carburetor
   (b) A decreasing manifold vacuum
   (c) A stuck open choke
   (d) Idle mixture screws set too rich
7. Which of these would result if the piston rings were installed upside down?
   (a) A high pitch rap or knock
   (b) Loss of compression
   (c) Broken ring lands
   (d) High oil consumption
8. The accelerator pump circuit is required because when the throttle is suddenly opened
   (a) Air moves faster than fuel
   (b) Air moves slower than fuel
   (c) Air and fuel move at the same speed
   (d) None of the above

9. One major difference between a two-cycle and a four-cycle engine is that a two-cycle engine does *not* have
   (a) A combustion chamber
   (b) A piston
   (c) Rings
   (d) Valves
10. An automatic transmission does not work right. To find the cause, which of these should the mechanic do *first*?
    (a) Take a pressure test.
    (b) Adjust the bands.
    (c) Check the transmission fluid.
    (d) Check engine vacuum.
11. In road testing a vehicle, you find that the steering wheel shakes from side to side at higher speeds. Mechanic A says this could be caused by front wheels not being statically balanced. Mechanic B says this could be caused by front wheels not being dynamically balanced. Who is right?
    (a) A only
    (b) B only
    (c) Either A or B
    (d) Neither A nor B
12. With the oil pan removed, the best way to pin-point an oil-pressure leak is to
    (a) Take a pump-pressure reading
    (b) Check line pressure
    (c) Remove and check the control body
    (d) Perform an air-pressure test
13. A car owner says the brake pedal moves slowly to the floor when holding the foot on the pedal. Which of the following could cause this problem?
    (a) Leaking primary piston cup
    (b) Defective power booster (leaking)
    (c) Leaking residual check valve
    (d) All the above
14. A modern V-8 engine consumes too much oil and idles rough. It is known that the rings and valves are good and properly installed. Which of these may be true?
    I. The intake manifold leaks.
    II. The exhaust manifold leaks.
    (a) I only
    (b) II only
    (c) Either I or II
    (d) Neither I nor II
15. Each of these problems will usually cause hard shifting into gear *except*
    (a) Clutch not releasing
    (b) Sliding gear loose on shaft splines
    (c) Shifter fork bent
    (d) Gearshift linkage out of adjustment
16. The mechanic finds raw gas (flooding) at the carburetor. Which of the following would *least* likely cause this problem?
    (a) Needle and seat defective
    (b) Plugged air bleeds
    (c) High fuel-pump pressure
    (d) Misaligned float

17. Excess negative caster on the left front wheel only will cause which of these to happen?
    I. The car will pull to the left.
    II. The left tire will wear on the outside edge of the tread.
    (a) I only
    (b) II only
    (c) Both I and II
    (d) Neither I nor II
18. Check valves are not used in master cylinders with disc brakes. Putting a check valve into a disc-brake system would cause which one of these symptoms?
    (a) Low brake pedal
    (b) Loss of brake fluid from system
    (c) Rapid wear of the pads
    (d) Run out of the rotor
19. Mechanic A says a noisy alternator could be caused by an open stator field. Mechanic B says a noisy alternator could be caused by a worn bearing. Who is right?
    (a) A only
    (b) B only
    (c) Either A or B
    (d) Neither A nor B
20. To test available voltage of the ignition coil with an oscilloscope, it is necessary to remove
    (a) Coil wire and ground on engine block
    (b) Primary wire to the coil
    (c) Spark plug wire and then ground it
    (d) Spark plug wire and then hold it from ground
21. The disc-brake part of a dual master cylinder is low on fluid. Mechanic A says the brake pads may be worn. Mechanic B says the power-brake booster may be faulty. Who is right?
    (a) A only
    (b) B only
    (c) Both A and B
    (d) Neither A nor B

Automotive Mechanics Test

Answer each of the following items by circling the correct answer. Answer every item. There is only one correct answer per item.

1. The circuit that controls the fuel level in the carburetor is the
   (a) Idle circuit
   (b) Float circuit
   (c) Power circuit
   (d) Choke circuit

2. A *stall test* can be used to check
   (a) Planetary gear noise
   (b) Governor pressure
   (c) Converter one-way clutch
   (d) Erratic shifting

3. The distributor shaft turns 360° for each time the engine rotates
   (a) 360°
   (b) 720°
   (c) 90°
   (d) 540°

4. Vapor lock is caused by
   (a) Using premium fuel
   (b) Too much heat on the fuel pump and lines
   (c) Too much fuel pump pressure
   (d) All the above

5. Which stroke of a four-cycle engine creates vacuum?
   (a) Intake
   (b) Exhaust
   (c) Compression
   (d) Power

6. Carburetor power circuits are *usually* brought into operation by
   (a) A decreasing fuel level in the carburetor
   (b) A decreasing manifold vacuum
   (c) A stuck open choke
   (d) Idle mixture screws set too rich

7. Which of these would result if the piston rings were installed upside down?
   (a) A high pitch rap or knock
   (b) Loss of compression
   (c) Broken ring lands
   (d) High oil consumption

8. The accelerator pump circuit is required because when the throttle is suddenly opened
   (a) Air moves faster than fuel
   (b) Air moves slower than fuel
   (c) Air and fuel move at the same speed
   (d) None of the above

9. One major difference between a two-cycle and a four-cycle engine is that a two-cycle engine does *not* have
   (a) A combustion chamber
   (b) A piston
   (c) Rings
   (d) Valves

10. An automatic transmission does not work right. To find the cause, which of these should the mechanic do *first*?
    (a) Take a pressure test.
    (b) Adjust the bands.
    (c) Check the transmission fluid.
    (d) Check engine vacuum.

11. In road testing a vehicle, you find that the steering wheel shakes from side to side at higher speeds. Mechanic A says this could be caused by front wheels not being statically balanced. Mechanic B says this could be caused by front wheels not being dynamically balanced. Who is right?
    (a) A only
    (b) B only
    (c) Either A or B
    (d) Neither A nor B

12. With the oil pan removed, the best way to pin-point an oil-pressure leak is to
    (a) Take a pump-pressure reading
    (b) Check line pressure
    (c) Remove and check the control body
    (d) Perform an air-pressure test

13. A car owner says the brake pedal moves slowly to the floor when holding the foot on the pedal. Which of the following could cause this problem?
    (a) Leaking primary piston cup
    (b) Defective power booster (leaking)
    (c) Leaking residual check valve
    (d) All the above

14. A modern V-8 engine consumes too much oil and idles rough. It is known that the rings and valves are good and properly installed. Which of these may be true?
    I. The intake manifold leaks.
    II. The exhaust manifold leaks.
    (a) I only
    (b) II only
    (c) Either I or II
    (d) Neither I nor II

15. Each of these problems will usually cause hard shifting into gear *except*
    (a) Clutch not releasing
    (b) Sliding gear loose on shaft splines
    (c) Shifter fork bent
    (d) Gearshift linkage out of adjustment

16. The mechanic finds raw gas (flooding) at the carburetor. Which of the following would *least* likely cause this problem?
    (a) Needle and seat defective
    (b) Plugged air bleeds
    (c) High fuel-pump pressure
    (d) Misaligned float

17. Excess negative caster on the left front wheel only will cause which of these to happen?
    I. The car will pull to the left.
    II. The left tire will wear on the outside edge of the tread.
    (a) I only
    (b) II only
    (c) Both I and II
    (d) Neither I nor II

18. Check valves are not used in master cylinders with disc brakes. Putting a check valve into a disc-brake system would cause which one of these symptoms?
    (a) Low brake pedal
    (b) Loss of brake fluid from system
    (c) Rapid wear of the pads
    (d) Run out of the rotor

19. Mechanic A says a noisy alternator could be caused by an open stator field. Mechanic B says a noisy alternator could be caused by a worn bearing. Who is right?
    (a) A only
    (b) B only
    (c) Either A or B
    (d) Neither A nor B

20. To test available voltage of the ignition coil with an oscilloscope, it is necessary to remove
    (a) Coil wire and ground on engine block
    (b) Primary wire to the coil
    (c) Spark plug wire and then ground it
    (d) Spark plug wire and then hold it from ground

21. The disc-brake part of a dual master cylinder is low on fluid. Mechanic A says the brake pads may be worn. Mechanic B says the power-brake booster may be faulty. Who is right?
    (a) A only
    (b) B only
    (c) Both A and B
    (d) Neither A nor B

Automotive Mechanics Test

Answer each of the following items by circling the correct answer. Answer every item. There is only one correct answer per item.

1. The circuit that controls the fuel level in the carburetor is the
    (a) Idle circuit
    (b) Float circuit
    (c) Power circuit
    (d) Choke circuit
2. A *stall test* can be used to check
    (a) Planetary gear noise
    (b) Governor pressure
    (c) Converter one-way clutch
    (d) Erratic shifting
3. The distributor shaft turns 360° for each time the engine rotates
    (a) 360°
    (b) 720°
    (c) 90°
    (d) 540°
4. Vapor lock is caused by
    (a) Using premium fuel
    (b) Too much heat on the fuel pump and lines
    (c) Too much fuel pump pressure
    (d) All the above
5. Which stroke of a four-cycle engine creates vacuum?
    (a) Intake
    (b) Exhaust
    (c) Compression
    (d) Power
6. Carburetor power circuits are *usually* brought into operation by
    (a) A decreasing fuel level in the carburetor
    (b) A decreasing manifold vacuum
    (c) A stuck open choke
    (d) Idle mixture screws set too rich
7. Which of these would result if the piston rings were installed upside down?
    (a) A high pitch rap or knock
    (b) Loss of compression
    (c) Broken ring lands
    (d) High oil consumption
8. The accelerator pump circuit is required because when the throttle is suddenly opened
    (a) Air moves faster than fuel
    (b) Air moves slower than fuel
    (c) Air and fuel move at the same speed
    (d) None of the above

9. One major difference between a two-cycle and a four-cycle engine is that a two-cycle engine does *not* have
   (a) A combustion chamber
   (b) A piston
   (c) Rings
   (d) Valves
10. An automatic transmission does not work right. To find the cause, which of these should the mechanic do *first*?
    (a) Take a pressure test.
    (b) Adjust the bands.
    (c) Check the transmission fluid.
    (d) Check engine vacuum.
11. In road testing a vehicle, you find that the steering wheel shakes from side to side at higher speeds. Mechanic A says this could be caused by front wheels not being statically balanced. Mechanic B says this could be caused by front wheels not being dynamically balanced. Who is right?
    (a) A only
    (b) B only
    (c) Either A or B
    (d) Neither A nor B
12. With the oil pan removed, the best way to pin-point an oil-pressure leak is to
    (a) Take a pump-pressure reading
    (b) Check line pressure
    (c) Remove and check the control body
    (d) Perform an air-pressure test
13. A car owner says the brake pedal moves slowly to the floor when holding the foot on the pedal. Which of the following could cause this problem?
    (a) Leaking primary piston cup
    (b) Defective power booster (leaking)
    (c) Leaking residual check valve
    (d) All the above
14. A modern V-8 engine consumes too much oil and idles rough. It is known that the rings and valves are good and properly installed. Which of these may be true?
     I. The intake manifold leaks.
    II. The exhaust manifold leaks.
    (a) I only
    (b) II only
    (c) Either I or II
    (d) Neither I nor II
15. Each of these problems will usually cause hard shifting into gear *except*
    (a) Clutch not releasing
    (b) Sliding gear loose on shaft splines
    (c) Shifter fork bent
    (d) Gearshift linkage out of adjustment
16. The mechanic finds raw gas (flooding) at the carburetor. Which of the following would *least* likely cause this problem?
    (a) Needle and seat defective
    (b) Plugged air bleeds
    (c) High fuel-pump pressure
    (d) Misaligned float

17. Excess negative caster on the left front wheel only will cause which of these to happen?
     I. The car will pull to the left.
     II. The left tire will wear on the outside edge of the tread.
     (a) I only
     (b) II only
     (c) Both I and II
     (d) Neither I nor II

18. Check valves are not used in master cylinders with disc brakes. Putting a check valve into a disc-brake system would cause which one of these symptoms?
     (a) Low brake pedal
     (b) Loss of brake fluid from system
     (c) Rapid wear of the pads
     (d) Run out of the rotor

19. Mechanic A says a noisy alternator could be caused by an open stator field. Mechanic B says a noisy alternator could be caused by a worn bearing. Who is right?
     (a) A only
     (b) B only
     (c) Either A or B
     (d) Neither A nor B

20. To test available voltage of the ignition coil with an oscilloscope, it is necessary to remove
     (a) Coil wire and ground on engine block
     (b) Primary wire to the coil
     (c) Spark plug wire and then ground it
     (d) Spark plug wire and then hold it from ground

21. The disc-brake part of a dual master cylinder is low on fluid. Mechanic A says the brake pads may be worn. Mechanic B says the power-brake booster may be faulty. Who is right?
     (a) A only
     (b) B only
     (c) Both A and B
     (d) Neither A nor B

Automotive Mechanics Test

Answer each of the following items by circling the correct answer. Answer every item. There is only one correct answer per item.

1. The circuit that controls the fuel level in the carburetor is the
   - (a) Idle circuit
   - (b) Float circuit
   - (c) Power circuit
   - (d) Choke circuit

2. A *stall test* can be used to check
   - (a) Planetary gear noise
   - (b) Governor pressure
   - (c) Converter one-way clutch
   - (d) Erratic shifting

3. The distributor shaft turns 360° for each time the engine rotates
   - (a) 360°
   - (b) 720°
   - (c) 90°
   - (d) 540°

4. Vapor lock is caused by
   - (a) Using premium fuel
   - (b) Too much heat on the fuel pump and lines
   - (c) Too much fuel pump pressure
   - (d) All the above

5. Which stroke of a four-cycle engine creates vacuum?
   - (a) Intake
   - (b) Exhaust
   - (c) Compression
   - (d) Power

6. Carburetor power circuits are *usually* brought into operation by
   - (a) A decreasing fuel level in the carburetor
   - (b) A decreasing manifold vacuum
   - (c) A stuck open choke
   - (d) Idle mixture screws set too rich

7. Which of these would result if the piston rings were installed upside down?
   - (a) A high pitch rap or knock
   - (b) Loss of compression
   - (c) Broken ring lands
   - (d) High oil consumption

8. The accelerator pump circuit is required because when the throttle is suddenly opened
   - (a) Air moves faster than fuel
   - (b) Air moves slower than fuel
   - (c) Air and fuel move at the same speed
   - (d) None of the above

9. One major difference between a two-cycle and a four-cycle engine is that a two-cycle engine does *not* have
(a) A combustion chamber
(b) A piston
(c) Rings
(d) Valves

10. An automatic transmission does not work right. To find the cause, which of these should the mechanic do *first*?
(a) Take a pressure test.
(b) Adjust the bands.
(c) Check the transmission fluid.
(d) Check engine vacuum.

11. In road testing a vehicle, you find that the steering wheel shakes from side to side at higher speeds. Mechanic A says this could be caused by front wheels not being statically balanced. Mechanic B says this could be caused by front wheels not being dynamically balanced. Who is right?
(a) A only
(b) B only
(c) Either A or B
(d) Neither A nor B

12. With the oil pan removed, the best way to pin-point an oil-pressure leak is to
(a) Take a pump-pressure reading
(b) Check line pressure
(c) Remove and check the control body
(d) Perform an air-pressure test

13. A car owner says the brake pedal moves slowly to the floor when holding the foot on the pedal. Which of the following could cause this problem?
(a) Leaking primary piston cup
(b) Defective power booster (leaking)
(c) Leaking residual check valve
(d) All the above

14. A modern V-8 engine consumes too much oil and idles rough. It is known that the rings and valves are good and properly installed. Which of these may be true?
I. The intake manifold leaks.
II. The exhaust manifold leaks.
(a) I only
(b) II only
(c) Either I or II
(d) Neither I nor II

15. Each of these problems will usually cause hard shifting into gear *except*
(a) Clutch not releasing
(b) Sliding gear loose on shaft splines
(c) Shifter fork bent
(d) Gearshift linkage out of adjustment

16. The mechanic finds raw gas (flooding) at the carburetor. Which of the following would *least* likely cause this problem?
(a) Needle and seat defective
(b) Plugged air bleeds
(c) High fuel-pump pressure
(d) Misaligned float

17. Excess negative caster on the left front wheel only will cause which of these to happen?
    I. The car will pull to the left.
    II. The left tire will wear on the outside edge of the tread.
    (a) I only
    (b) II only
    (c) Both I and II
    (d) Neither I nor II

18. Check valves are not used in master cylinders with disc brakes. Putting a check valve into a disc-brake system would cause which one of these symptoms?
    (a) Low brake pedal
    (b) Loss of brake fluid from system
    (c) Rapid wear of the pads
    (d) Run out of the rotor

19. Mechanic A says a noisy alternator could be caused by an open stator field. Mechanic B says a noisy alternator could be caused by a worn bearing. Who is right?
    (a) A only
    (b) B only
    (c) Either A or B
    (d) Neither A nor B

20. To test available voltage of the ignition coil with an oscilloscope, it is necessary to remove
    (a) Coil wire and ground on engine block
    (b) Primary wire to the coil
    (c) Spark plug wire and then ground it
    (d) Spark plug wire and then hold it from ground

21. The disc-brake part of a dual master cylinder is low on fluid. Mechanic A says the brake pads may be worn. Mechanic B says the power-brake booster may be faulty. Who is right?
    (a) A only
    (b) B only
    (c) Both A and B
    (d) Neither A nor B

Answer Key for Automotive Mechanics Test

1. b
2. c
3. b
4. b
5. a
6. b
7. d
8. a
9. d
10. c
11. c
12. d
13. a
14. a
15. b
16. b
17. a
18. c
19. b
20. d
21. a

LABORATORY EXERCISE 16

Diagnosis
of Learning Disabilities

PURPOSE

The purpose of this exercise is to give the class members experience in some of the problems of diagnosing learning disabilities. Due to the sensitive nature of this topic, you will not actually administer tests to children. A description of a child experiencing some difficulties in school will be presented, and you will select a battery of tests to be used for diagnostic purposes. You will describe the rationale for each test, the types of information expected and subsequent actions to be taken with the results. Furthermore, you will be expected to use information on reliability and validity you have learned in previous chapters. The purpose of this exercise is *not* to train you in the skills necessary to diagnose a learning disability, but only to acquaint you with some of the basic problems involved in a diagnosis.

OVERVIEW

Children with learning disabilities do not profit from traditional instruction in specific academic areas such as reading, spelling, or mathematics, even though they have the potential and the opportunity to learn. Accurate diagnosis is essential for a number of reasons. First, it alerts educators that these children need some kind of special help. Accurate diagnosis also helps determine which treatment or program would be most appropriate for the child. For example, learning disabled children are often confused with emotionally and behaviorally disturbed children, even though treatment in the first case would be primarily educational and in the second case primarily psychological. Finally, diagnosis helps identify the child's areas of deficiency and is, therefore, crucial in developing strategies for teaching the child some basic learning skills.

KEY PRINCIPLES FOR TEST SELECTION

In selecting tests for a diagnostic battery, there are two general requirements that must be fulfilled. First, each test must be reliable and valid for the diagnostic purposes, and second, each test must be appropriate for the individual who is being tested. For each standardized test, it is important that good, normative data exist and that these data are appropriate for the subject's age, sex, and background. Furthermore, the test should have been demonstrated to be an accurate measure of the constructs the diagnostician wishes to measure. Finally, the diagnostician should take into account not only the test's general validity but also its discriminant validity, that is, whether this test has been previously demonstrated to be independent of other tests being used. In the absence of past studies of discriminant validity, it may be necessary to learn what types of items are used on the test and compare these to the items used on other tests in the diagnostic battery. Sometimes, tests which are supposed to measure very different constructs are in fact quite similar. When this is the case, discriminant validity is suspect. However, if two tests have similar labels but include very different types of items, the validity of one of the tests may be questionable.

 The second set of requirements for a good diagnostic test considers whether or not it is appropriate for the learning disabled individual. Some tests, which are reliable and valid measures for normal (typical) individuals, fail to measure the desired construct for the learning disabled population. A test composed of written "story" problems may measure mathematic skills for a typical student. However, for a student who has poor reading skills, this test would become little more than a reading test. For this reason, many group intelligence tests and achievement tests are inappropriate for the learning disabled individual because they rely so heavily on reading. Furthermore, many learning disabled students have poor verbal skills, thus rendering some traditional intelligence tests inappropriate. Other intelligence tests which have nonverbal or performance sections may be more helpful in providing a valid picture of the student's true abilities. Finally, in determining appropriate tests, the diagnostician must select tests which will supply usable, prescriptive information for remediating the problems that the subject demonstrates. For example, on some achievement tests it is possible to record the types of mistakes the subject makes. This information helps determine the concepts or skills that the child needs to be taught.

GUIDELINES FOR DIAGNOSING A LEARNING DISABILITY

Because the field of learning disabilities is relatively new, there are many definitions of what constitutes a learning disability. However, one of the most useful definitions states that *individuals with specific learning disabilities demonstrate a significant discrepancy between expected and actual achievement, with significant deficits in essential learning processes not primarily the result of sensory, motor, intellectual, or emotional handicaps or a lack of opportunity to learn.*

This definition is composed of three basic parts. The first part can be called the "significant discrepancy" clause. The discrepancy may be in one or more areas such as math, reading, speaking, or writing. The discrepancy between expected ability and actual achievement is measured, using appropriate intelligence and achievement tests. This means that most diagnostic batteries for a learning disability begin by administering an intelligence test and an achievement test, and then comparing the results.

The second part of the definition deals with "essential learning processes." Learning disabled individuals demonstrate one or more significant deficits in learning processes such as perception, integration of information, and verbal or motor expression. The perceptual deficits mentioned might include:

Auditory Discrimination. The ability to distinguish small differences in the tone, timbre, or intensity of sounds. A student with poor auditory discrimination may have normal hearing acuity but may be called "word deaf" because similar sounds or words often sound exactly alike.

Auditory Memory. The ability to remember sounds in sequence. Poor spelling may result from poor auditory memory. The student with a weak auditory memory may also fail to retain words or sentences spoken in sequence, such as oral directions or commands.

Visual Discrimination. The ability to distinguish small differences in visual stimuli, especially in two-dimensional symbols. A student with poor visual discrimination may have normal vision but may be said to be "word blind" because similar words or letters often look alike.

Visual Memory. The ability to retain the visual image of a two-dimensional symbol, especially the sequence of symbols in whole words, or the sequence of words in phrases and sentences. Poor reading or poor spelling may result from a weak visual memory.

Integration deficits may include visual-motor integration, that is, the ability to translate visual patterns into motor patterns. Students with poor visual-motor integration may experience difficulty in copying or in handwriting. Finally, learning disabled students may demonstrate deficits in verbal or motor expression. Verbal expression includes spoken and written language whereas motor expression includes gross and fine motor coordination.

Because a significant discrepancy between expected and actual achievement or deficits in the essential learning process can have several causes, the last section of the definition states that learning disabilities are "not primarily the result of sensory, motor, intellectual, or emotional handicaps or lack of opportunity to learn." To eliminate these plausible explanations, the diagnostician must investigate many other important features in the child's early life, home environment, and school situation.

Given this definition, the diagnostician must first, document a discrepancy between the child's ability and achievement; second, demonstrate one or more deficits in essential learning processes, such as auditory discrimination, auditory memory, visual discrimination, visual memory, visual-motor integration, oral or written expression, or fine or gross motor coordination; and finally, make sure that these discrepancies and deficits are not caused by blindness, deafness, intellectual or emotional handicaps, or a lack of opportunity to learn in the home or school.

NOTICE

The diagnosis of a learning disability is a very complicated procedure. The present exercise has been simplified to provide an educational experience. It is *not* meant to be comprehensive training in the diagnosis of learning disabilities.

PROCEDURES

1. Read the case material.
2. Prepare a tentative diagnosis: After reading the case material, make some educated guesses as to whether a learning disability is involved and in which areas there may be deficits. List these on the worksheet under the title "Tentative Disorders."
3. List the constructs to be measured: List the constructs that are to be measured by the diagnostic battery. In order to document a significant discrepancy between ability and achievement, the student should choose measures of the constructs of intelligence and achievement. With achievement, it is important to specify which areas. Furthermore, the diagnostician must also measure at least one of the essential learning processes to demonstrate a deficit in one of those areas.
4. Review sources: In order to find tests for the diagnostic battery, students should use the reference section of the library. One useful resource in test selection is *Tests in Print II* (1974) by O. K. Buros (ed.). In this volume, students can look in the following sections to find tests which measure the desired constructs:
   a. Intelligence tests
   b. Achievement tests
   c. Sensory and motor tests
   d. Hearing and speech tests
   e. Miscellaneous—learning disabilities
   Once the tests have been selected, more information about them can be obtained using *Mental Measurements Yearbook* (1978) by O. K. Buros and *Reading Tests and Reviews* (1968) by O. K. Buros. The earlier volumes are more likely to include statistical information on reliability and validity. Many tests may not have information on reliability and validity. However, this is important information in selecting a test; so when possible, use tests for which there is evidence of reliability and validity. More information may be available by looking under "learning disabilities" in the card file. Your instructor may also provide some resource material.
5. Select tests: Constructs can be measured either by separate tests or by an integrated test battery which measures more than one construct. Table 16.1 contains a list of possible tests. However, the student is encouraged to also use other sources because this list is limited and new tests are continuously being developed. In selecting each test, pay particular attention to the reliability and validity data. Each test should be listed on the worksheet.
6. State rationale and defense of each test: Under each test, the student should explain the rationale for the use of that test and defend its reliability, validity, and appropriateness for the child being assessed.
7. State anticipated results of testing, recommendations, and payoffs: In this section, the student should state some reasonable guesses about the test results, write down these hypothetical findings, and make appropriate recommendations if these results were obtained. Finally, the student should list the possible benefits that would result from administering the test battery. For example, if you decide the problem is not emotional but a learning disability, this information would help the child's teachers understand his or her behavior and possibly rearrange the classroom so that the child can hear or see better or be less distracted by disruptions, if these are in fact problems for the child.

SUGGESTED READINGS

Anastasi, A. *Psychological Testing* (4th ed.). New York: Macmillan, 1976, pp. 417–422.

Brown, F. G. *Principles of Educational and Psychological Testing* (2nd ed.). New York: Holt, Rinehart and Winston, 1976, pp. 287–290.

Cronbach, L. J. *Essentials of Psychological Testing* (3rd ed.). New York: Harper & Row, 1970, pp. 248–251.

Gronlund N. E. *Measurement and Evaluation in Teaching* (3rd ed.). New York: Macmillan, 1976, pp. 494–499.

Thorndike, R. L., and Hagan, E. *Measurement and Evaluation in Psychology and Education* (4th ed.). New York: Wiley, 1977, pp. 166–177.

Table 16.1 A Partial List of Tests Appropriate for Diagnostic Purposes

Intelligence Tests

Arthur Point Scale of Performance Test
Peabody Picture Vocabulary Test
The Porteous Maze Test
Stanford Binet Intelligence Test
Wechsler Intelligence Scale for Children (revised)
Raven Progressive Matrices

Achievement Tests

California Achievement Tests
The Gray-Votaw-Rogers General Achievement Tests
The Metropolitan Achievement Tests
Peabody Individual Achievement Test
Stanford Achievement Test
Wide Range Achievement Test, Revised Edition

Tests of Essential Learning Processes

Auditory Discrimination
    Goldman-Fistoe-Woodcock Test of Auditory Discrimination
    Lindamood Auditory Conceptualization Test
    Oliphant Auditory Discrimination Memory Test
    Pritchard-Fox Phoneme Auditory Discrimination Tests
    Rush-Hughes: Phonetically Balanced Lists 5-12
Visual Memory
    Specific Language Disability Test
        (Visual perceptual memory for words)
    Detroit Tests of Learning Aptitude
        (Visual attention span)
    Benton Visual Retention Test
Visual-motor Integration
    Bender Gestalt Test
    Developmental Test of Visual-Motor Integration

CASE MATERIAL

Peter was referred to the clinic by his physician because of learning and behavioral difficulties. Peter was a 12-year-old in the sixth grade. He had an older and younger sister. The physician reported that Peter had a problem-free birth and infancy with no serious illnesses or injuries. Furthermore, Peter was in excellent health and had just completed a visual and auditory screening which demonstrated that he had normal acuity.

Peter's father is a successful architect, and Peter's mother completed a college education. Both parents reported that although Peter's speech developed late, he appeared to be a bright, affectionate child. At the age of 6, Peter seemed to become far more aggressive than earlier, particularly with his two sisters, and spent more time playing alone. His greatest problems at home were following directions and expressing himself. When telling a story, Peter had great difficulty in describing the important events in sequence. Furthermore, many times Peter could not remember the word that he wished to use. This caused him much frustration, and Peter would stamp off in anger. However, his parents observed that he loves to fix things, such as bicycles or old radios and appears remarkably talented at these tasks.

Peter's school is located in the suburbs of a large city and is an excellent facility with a low student-to-teacher ratio. The school records indicate that Peter experienced little difficulty until the end of the first grade. However, Peter's performance in second grade was so poor he had to repeat it. Peter's school history consisted of poor academic performance and behavioral problems. His sixth grade teacher summarized his performance:

> Peter's reading is significantly below his grade level. In silent reading, he is slow and demonstrates little comprehension. In oral reading, he reverses letters such as "b" and "d" and confuses similar words. In spelling, Peter has similar difficulties. He reverses letters and is unable to tell the difference between vowel sounds. His handwriting is very poor, and he has difficulty copying geometric designs. However, Peter's performance in mathematics and physical education is at grade level, and he enjoys these activities.
>
> Behaviorally, Peter's favorite activity is playing or working alone in a quiet environment. He has a low level of tolerance for frustration, and when faced with failure, he tends to become aggressive. When other children approach him, Peter will strike out at them and often get into fights. In general, Peter is failing both the academic and social aspects of school.

The school's social worker reported that Peter's home life appeared normal. His parents have been able to provide both affection and structure. Using projective tests, the school psychologist found no evidence of severe emotional or behavioral problems.

Worksheet for Diagnosis

Tentative disorders

Constructs to be measured

Sources consulted

Tests to be given and rationale

Anticipated results, recommendations, and payoffs

LABORATORY EXERCISE A

Statistical Concepts and Procedures 1: Frequency Distributions; Mean, Median, and Mode; Percentiles

PURPOSE

The purpose of this exercise is to review a number of concepts and techniques the student has learned in elementary statistics. First, sets of scores are arranged in frequency distributions. With the data grouped in this manner, the mean, median, and mode of each distribution should be computed. Next, the scores are converted to percentiles.

DATA COLLECTION

The students in the class are asked to make individual judgments about the height and weight and to guess the score on a college aptitude test of 20 other individuals. Standards for estimating test scores appear in Table A.1. For example, if the estimate is that an individual would be in the top 16 percent, the test score would be 625.

The first student in a row is asked to stand; the rest of the students estimate height, weight, and test score, entering these estimates in Table A.2. A second student is asked to stand, and the estimates are repeated up to 20 sets of estimates. The standing student also estimates his or her own scores.

The instructor may provide students with sets of scores as an alternative to the above procedure.

FREQUENCY DISTRIBUTIONS

To assist in the interpretation of a distribution of scores and to reduce the work in computing certain statistics, it is advantageous to arrange the scores in a frequency distribution. A frequency distribution is an arrangement of the data which shows the frequency of different values or groups of values of the variable.

Frequency distributions for the estimates of height (Table A.3), weight (Table A.4), and college aptitude test scores (Table A.5) are provided.

MEAN, MEDIAN, AND MODE

The scores may be tabulated for each distribution and the mean, median, and mode computed. The formula for the mean with ungrouped data is

$$\overline{X} = \frac{\Sigma X}{N}$$

where X stands for the individual scores, Σ for "the sum of," and N for the total number of scores or measures. With grouped data, the formula is

$$\overline{X} = \frac{\Sigma f X}{N}$$

where f stands for the frequency of measures in each group, and X stands for the midpoint of each group or class interval.

The *median* is the midpoint of a distribution of scores arranged in order of magnitude, or the point above and below which lie 50 percent of the scores. With ungrouped data the median is found by dividing N by 2 and counting up from the bottom of the distribution to the point which has this number of scores below it. With grouped data, we follow the same procedure. However, we can also use the formula

$$\text{Mdn} = 1.00 + \left(\frac{\frac{N}{2} - \Sigma f_b}{f_w} \right) i$$

where l stands for the lower limit of the group wherein the middle score lies, f_b for the sum of the frequencies below that group, f_w for the frequency in that group, and i for the size of the group.

The *mode* is the score which occurs most frequently. In group data, the mode is the midpoint of the class interval containing the most scores.

PERCENTILES

The most common method of comparison of test scores is by use of percentiles. A *percentile* is a value on a scale below which fall a given percentage of the cases. Percentiles show the position of a given score in a distribution of scores. For example, if a score is at the 20th percentile, that score is greater than 20 percent of the scores. The 90th percentile refers to the score which is greater than 90 percent of the other scores.

Percentiles are easily understood. They allow comparison of scores from different distributions. Their disadvantage is that they cannot be combined by averaging or most other statistical manipulation. Percentiles are not equal units of measure. For most exercises in this workbook, percentile ranks will be computed because they are easy to compute. *Percentile ranks* are approximations of percentiles and will suffice to illustrate measurement principles.

In this exercise, percentile ranks are computed for height, weight, and college aptitude test scores.

PROCEDURE

1. In the frequency column, record the number of people scoring at each level.
2. Tabulate these scores by writing down the ranks of the scores from the low to high scores.
3. The *average rank* is simply the average of the numbers in that raw score category.
4. Divide the average rank by the total number of cases to find the percentile rank.

An illustration of this procedure is given in Figure A.1.

Raw Score	Frequency	Tabulate	Average Rank	Percentile Rank
"				
"				
"				
5'5"	3	6,7,8	7	35
5'4"	2	4,5	4.5	22.5
5'3"	1	3	3	15
5'2"	2	1,2	1.5	7.5
		Total $N = 20$		

Figure A.1   Illustration of Computation of Percentile Ranks

SUGGESTED READINGS

Anastasi, A. *Psychological Testing* (4th ed.). New York: Macmillan, 1976, pp. 68–71, 78–80.

Brown, F. G. *Principles of Educational and Psychological Testing* (2nd ed.). New York: Holt, Rinehart and Winston, 1976, pp. 36–38, 180–183.

Cronbach, L. J. *Essentials of Psychological Testing* (3rd ed.). New York: Harper & Row, 1970, pp. 89–94.

Gronlund, N. E. *Measurement and Evaluation in Teaching* (3rd ed.). New York: Macmillan, 1976, pp. 398–401, 539–553.

Mehrens, W. A., and Lehmann, I. J. *Measurement and Evaluation in Education and Psychology* (2nd ed.). New York: Holt, Rinehart and Winston, 1975, pp. 76–79, 143–144.

Thorndike, R. L., and Hagan, E. *Measurement and Evaluation in Psychology and Education* (4th ed.). New York: Wiley, 1977, pp. 33–40, 124–137.

Table A.1 Standards for Estimating Scores on a College
Aptitude Test

Standards for Estimating Scores on a College Aptitude Test

690	Upper	5%
650	Upper	10%
625	Upper	16%
600	Upper	25%
580	Upper	33%
500		Average
420	Lower	33%
400	Lower	25%
375	Lower	16%
350	Lower	10%
310	Lower	5%

Table A.2 Table for Recording Estimates of Student Data

Number	Name	Height	Weight	College Aptitude Test
1				
2				
3				
4				
5				
6				
7				
8				
9				
10				
11				
12				
13				
14				
15				
16				
17				
18				
19				
20				

Table A.3 Height Distribution

Raw Score Height	Frequency	Tabulation	Average Rank	Percentile Rank (average rank/total N times 100)
6'3"				
6'2"				
6'1"				
6'0"				
5'11"				
5'10"				
5'9"				
5'8"				
5'7"				
5'6"				
5'5"				
5'4"				
5'3"				
5'2"				
5'1"				
5'0"				
4'11"				
4'10"				
4'9"				

Mode =
Median =
Mean =

Table A.4 Weight Distribution

Raw Score Weight	Frequency	Tabulation	Average Rank	Percentile
201+				
191–200				
181–190				
171–180				
161–170				
151–160				
141–150				
131–140				
121–130				
111–120				
101–100				
91–100				
81– 90				

Mode =
Median =
Mean =

Table A.5 College Test-Score Distribution

Raw Score college aptitude	Frequency	Tabulation	Average Rank	Percentile Rank
701+				
681–700				
661–680				
641–660				
621–640				
601–620				
581–600				
561–580				
541–560				
521–540				
501–520				
481–500				
461–480				
441–460				
421–440				
401–420				
381–400				
361–380				
341–360				
321–340				
301–320				

Mode   =
Median =
Mean   =

Assignment for **EXERCISE A**

1. Compute the mean, median, and mode for the estimates of height, weight, and score on the college aptitude test.
2. Compute the percentile ranks for the scores in the three distributions.
3. Answer the following questions:
   a. What are the differences between the *mean, median,* and *mode*?

   b. Define *percentile* and *percentile rank*.

   c. "Pat is 5'5" tall and weighs 130 pounds." How does Pat compare with the class? What other information would you want to have about Pat to know whether Pat was tall or short, heavy or light?

LABORATORY EXERCISE B

Statistical Concepts and Procedures II: Standard Deviation and Standard Scores

PURPOSE

This exercise covers the standard deviation and standard scores. Data from Exercise A can be used, or the instructor will provide sets of scores.

STANDARD DEVIATION

The *standard deviation* is a measure of variability of the scores around the mean. It is an indication of whether the scores are very similar to each other or very different. The standard deviation is a measure of how "spread out" the scores are.

In words, the standard deviation is the square root of the mean of squared deviations from the mean. That is, we (1) find the difference between each score and the mean, (2) square those differences, (3) sum up the squared differences, and (4) divide by the number of cases.

The formula reads

$$SD_x = \frac{\Sigma(X - \overline{X})^2}{N}$$

Table B.1 is used for the computation.

1. Record the height estimates (in inches) for the 20 subjects in Exercise A in the X column.
2. Compute the mean by summing scores and dividing by N.
3. In the column headed $(X - \overline{X})$, record the difference between each individual's height and the mean.
4. Find the square of each deviation and sum them.
5. Divide this sum by N and take the square root.
6. An alternative formula is provided for the direct computation of the standard deviation without computing the mean. In this formula, the square of each individual score (X^2) is found and used in the alternative formula.

STANDARD SCORE

A *standard score* is one method of comparing scores with each other. A standard score tells how far above or below the mean each score is, in terms of standard deviation units. For example, in a distribution of scores, one person may be two standard deviations above the mean, and a second person may be 1.5 standard deviations below the mean.

The computation of the standard score is very simple. After finding the standard deviation, the standard score is computed by subtracting each score from the mean and dividing by the standard deviation.

$$S = \frac{X - \overline{X}}{SD_x}$$

There are various types of standard scores. Any score can be converted to a standard score if the mean and standard deviation are known. A commonly used type of standard score is the z-score equivalent of any raw score is

$$z = \frac{X - \overline{X}}{SD_x}$$

Another commonly used type of standard score is the T score, which has a mean of 50 and a standard deviation of 10. Other familiar standard scores include the College Entrance Examination Board system with mean equal to 500 and standard deviation equal to 100, and the deviation IQ scores of the Stanford-Binet Intelligence Scale with a mean equal to 100 and standard deviation equal to 16.

RELATIONSHIP OF STANDARD SCORES AND PERCENTILES

Standard scores indicate a person's position in a distribution of scores by reference to the mean and standard deviation. When the raw scores are normally distributed, and we convert them to standard scores, the standard scores are related to percentiles in a very precise way. Because mathematicians and statisticians know the characteristics of the normal curve, we can make comparisons of standard scores and percentiles. Figure B.1 shows some comparisons. Additional comparisons can be found in tables of the normal curve found in most statistics books.

From these sources, we can make a conversion from standard scores to percentiles or the reverse. For example, a z score of 0.0 equals the 50th percentile, a z score of 1.0 equals the 84th percentile, and a z score of −1.0 equals the 16th percentile.

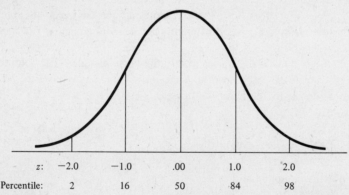

z:	−2.0	−1.0	.00	1.0	2.0
Percentile:	2	16	50	84	98

Figure B.1 Normal Curve and Selected Comparisons of Z Scores and Percentiles

SUGGESTED READINGS

Anastasi, A. *Psychological Testing* (4th ed.). New York: Macmillan, 1976, pp. 72–73, 80–88.

Brown, F. G. *Principles of Educational and Psychological Testing* (2nd ed.). New York: Holt, Rinehart and Winston, 1976, pp. 39–42, 184–190.

Cronbach, L. J. *Essentials of Psychological Testing* (3rd ed.). New York: Harper & Row, 1970, pp. 94–101.

Gronlund, N. E. *Measurement and Evaluation in Teaching* (3rd ed.). New York: Macmillan, 1976, pp. 543–545, 551–553.

Mehrens, W. A., and Lehmann, I. J. *Measurement and Evaluation in Education and Psychology* (2nd ed.). New York: Holt, Rinehart and Winston, 1975, pp. 79–81, 145–147.

Thorndike, R. L., and Hagan, E. *Measurement and Evaluation in Psychology and Education* (4th ed.). New York: Wiley, 1977, pp. 40–46, 129–137.

Table B.1 Computational Form for Standard Deviation

Subject	X	$X - \bar{X}$	$(X - \bar{X})^2$
1			
2			
3			
4			
5			
6			
7			
8			
9			
10			
11			
12			
13			
14			
15			
16			
17			
18			
19			
20			

$$\Sigma X = \qquad\qquad \Sigma(X - \bar{X})^2 =$$

$$\bar{X} = \frac{\Sigma X}{N}$$

$$\bar{X} =$$

$$SD_x = \sqrt{\frac{\Sigma(X - \bar{X})^2}{N}}$$

Alternative formula: $SD_x = \sqrt{\dfrac{\Sigma X^2 - \dfrac{(\Sigma X)^2}{N}}{N}}$

Name _____

Assignment for **EXERCISE B**

1. Compute the standard deviation for the height estimates using the method assigned by your instructor.
2. Pick two subjects and compute the z scores for these individuals' height estimates.
3. Answer the following questions:
   a. Define *standard deviation* in your own words.

   b. What is a *standard score*?

   c. Consult a table in a statistics book and find the percentile score corresponding to the following standard scores:

Standard Score (z)	Percentile
− .5	
.25	
1.20	

LABORATORY EXERCISE C

Statistical Concepts and Procedures III: Correlation—Spearman Rank-Difference and Pearson Product-Moment Procedures

PURPOSE

The purpose of this exercise is to review two techniques of correlation. Scatter diagrams are plotted and correlations are computed so that the student can see the relationship between these methods of representing a relationship between two variables.

CORRELATION

Correlational techniques are methods for investigating the relationship between two sets of scores for a sample of subjects. *The correlation coefficient* is a number which tells us to what extent two things covary, that is to what extent variations in one go with variations in the other. The correlation coefficient is a single number which expresses the magnitude and direction of the relationship. The coefficient is an index which ranges in size from $+1.00$ to -1.00. The size of the index expresses the magnitude of the relationship: 0.00 indicating no relationship. 0.30 to 0.50 indicating moderate relationship, and 0.80 to 1.00 indicating very strong relationship. The sign ($+$ or $-$) of the coefficient tells the direction of the relationship: a $+$ sign indicates a positive or direct relation, and a $-$ sign indicates a negative or inverse relation. There are many types of correlational techniques. Each technique has different applicability depending, in part, on the kind of data, the number of subjects, and the use that is to be made of the resulting information. The most common correlation reported is the Pearson product-moment correlation. This correlation uses standard scores in its computation so that the means and standard deviations of the two distributions are equated. One of the simpler methods for obtaining a correlation coefficient is the Spearman rank-difference method. This method is recommended for use in the exercises in this workbook. It has the advantage of being easy to graph and to compute without the use of calculators. It also provides a close estimate of the product-moment correlation.

DATA COLLECTION AND COMPUTATIONS
OF SPEARMAN RANK-DIFFERENCE CORRELATION

The student should use data collected in Exercise A. The computation of the rank-difference correlation coefficient (Spearman rho) can be carried out in Table C.1. Here, the student can record the rank order of the height estimates (from low to high) and the rank order of the weight estimate for each student. The difference between these two ranks for each student is then computed and recorded in the d column. The next steps are to square these values (d^2) and sum them in the last column. The correlation coefficient is computed with the formula written below the table. In the formula, N equals the number of subjects for whom you have the two sets of test data.

A scatter diagram of the data in Table C.1 can be shown in Figure C.1 by plotting on the graph a point corresponding to the rank on height and the rank on weight for each student. The *scatter diagram* is a chart which shows at a glance the overall pattern of relationships between two sets of scores. The scatter diagram can show the investigator many things about the relationship, for example, curvilinearity and different degrees of relationship in different portions of the diagram that are not apparent in the correlation coefficient.

The correlation coefficient and scatter diagram showing the relationship of the estimates of height and college aptitude score can be worked out in Table C.2 and Figure C.2, respectively.

PEARSON PRODUCT-MOMENT CORRELATION COEFFICIENT

The most widely used method of establishing the relationship between two variables is the Pearson product-moment correlation. In this exercise, two methods of computing the Pearson correlation coefficient (r) are illustrated: (1) the z score method and (2) the direct method, which can be facilitated with the use of a calculator.

Z SCORE METHOD

While this method is rather laborious, it is conceptually enlightening to see the correlation coefficient computed in this fashion. The basic formula is:

$$r = \frac{\Sigma z_x z_y}{N}$$

which defines the correlation as the mean of the product of the z scores. This formula illustrates that the two distributions of raw scores are equated for means and standard deviations by conversion to z scores in order to compute r.

The computation of the correlation can be carried out in Table C.3. The data for 20 subjects on two variables, namely, height and weight, from Exercise A should be recorded in the first two columns. After the mean of the height estimates ($\overline{X}$) is found, the x scores are computed from the following formula: $x = X - \overline{X}$. Next, the standard deviation of the X scores (SD_x) is computed: the x scores are squared and recorded in the appropriate column, and the square root of the mean of the x^2 values gives SD_x:

$$SD_x = \sqrt{\frac{\Sigma x^2}{N}}$$

The z_x values are found next by dividing each x by s. These z_x values express the original raw scores on the X variable in terms of mean of 0 and standard deviation of 1.

The y, y^2, s_y, and z_y values for the weight estimates should now be computed. The z_y values express the original raw scores on the Y variable in terms of mean of 0 and standard deviation of 1.

The next step is to multiply the z_x score and the z_y score for each individual subject. The sum of these products is divided by N to give r.

DIRECT METHOD

The direct method of the Pearson r utilizes the formula:

$$r = \frac{N\Sigma XY - (\Sigma X)(\Sigma Y)}{\sqrt{[N\Sigma X^2 - (\Sigma X)^2][N\Sigma Y^2 - (\Sigma Y)^2]}}$$

This seemingly awesome formula is, in reality, a relatively simple derivative of the z score formula the student used previously.

326

$$r_{xy} = \frac{\Sigma z_x z_y}{N}$$

Since

$$z_x = \frac{x}{s_x} \text{ and } z_y = \frac{y}{s_y}$$

then

$$r = \frac{\Sigma xy}{N s_x s_y}$$

Since

$$s_x = \sqrt{\frac{\Sigma x^2}{N}} \text{ and } s_y = \sqrt{\frac{\Sigma y^2}{N}}$$

then

$$r = \frac{\Sigma xy}{\sqrt{(\Sigma x^2)(\Sigma y^2)}}$$

Since

$$\Sigma x^2 = \Sigma X^2 - \frac{(\Sigma X)^2}{N}$$

$$\Sigma y^2 = \Sigma Y^2 - \frac{(\Sigma Y)^2}{N}$$

and

$$\Sigma xy = \Sigma XY - \frac{(\Sigma X)(\Sigma Y)}{N}$$

$$r = \frac{\Sigma XY - \dfrac{(\Sigma X)(\Sigma Y)}{N}}{\sqrt{\left[\Sigma X^2 - \dfrac{(\Sigma X^2)}{N}\right]\left[\Sigma Y^2 - \dfrac{(\Sigma Y^2)}{N}\right]}}$$

then

$$r = \frac{N\Sigma XY - \Sigma X \Sigma Y}{\sqrt{[N\Sigma X^2 - (\Sigma X)^2][N\Sigma Y^2 - (\Sigma Y)^2]}}$$

The same data in Table C.3 can be used for this method and can be recorded in Table C.4. The student should complete the data called for at the bottom of the table and find r.

SUGGESTED READINGS

Anastasi, A. *Psychological Testing* (4th ed.). New York: Macmillan, 1976, pp. 104–110.

Brown, F. G. *Principles of Educational and Psychological Testing* (2nd ed.). New York: Holt, Rinehart and Winston, 1976, pp. 42–45.

Cronbach, L. J. *Essentials of Psychological Testing* (3rd ed.). New York: Harper & Row, 1970, pp. 128–135.

Gronlund, N. E. *Measurement and Evaluation in Teaching* (3rd ed.). New York: Macmillan, 1976, pp. 85–88, 553–556.

Mehrens, W. A., and Lehmann, I. J. *Measurement and Evaluation in Education and Psychology* (2nd ed.). New York: Holt, Rinehart and Winston, 1975, pp. 81–85.

Thorndike, R. L., and Hagan, E. *Measurement and Evaluation in Psychology and Education* (4th ed.). New York: Wiley, 1977, pp. 47–52.

Name _____

Table C.1 Computation of Spearman Rank-Difference Correlation

Subject's Number	Height Rank Order	Weight Rank Order	d	d^2

$$\text{rho} = 1.00 - \frac{6\Sigma d^2}{N^3 - N}$$

$\Sigma d^2 =$ _____

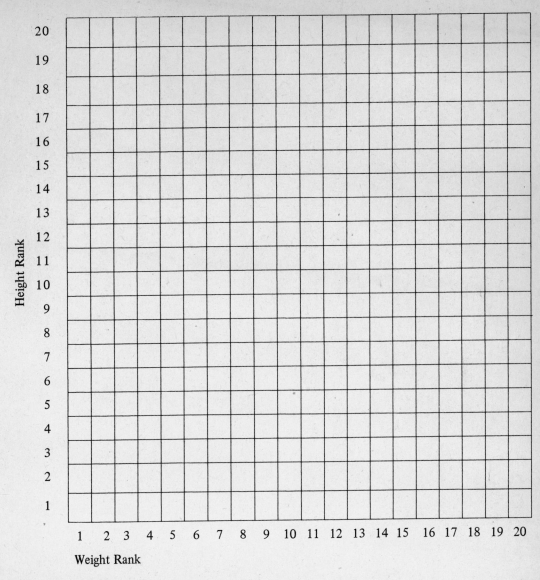

rho =

Figure C.1 Scatter Plot of Points

Table C.2 Computation of Spearman Rank-Difference Correlation

Subject's Number	Height Rank Order	College Aptitude Test Rank Order	d	d^2

$$\Sigma d^2 = \rule{3cm}{0.4pt}$$

$$\text{rho} = 1.00 - \frac{6\Sigma d^2}{N^3 - N}$$

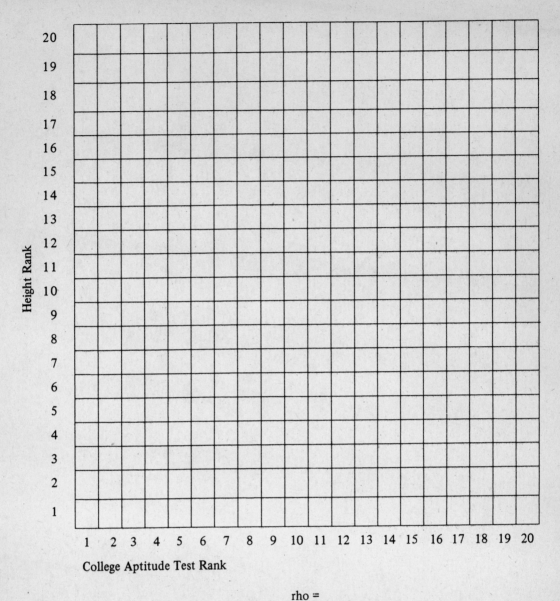

rho =

Figure C.2   Scatter Plot of Points

Name _____

Table C.3 Computation of Pearson r by z Score Method

Subject	X	Y	x	y	x^2	y^2	z_x	z_y	$z_x z_y$
1									
2									
3									
4									
5									
6									
7									
8									
9									
10									
11									
12									
13									
14									
15									
16									
17									
18									
19									
20									

$$\Sigma X = \qquad \Sigma Y = \qquad\qquad \Sigma x^2 = \quad \Sigma y^2 = \qquad\qquad \Sigma z_x z_y =$$

$$\bar{X} = \Sigma X / N =$$

$$\bar{Y} = \Sigma Y / N =$$

$$s_x = \sqrt{\frac{\Sigma x^2}{N}} =$$

$$s_y = \sqrt{\frac{\Sigma y^2}{N}} =$$

$$z_x = \frac{X - \bar{X}}{s_x} =$$

$$z_y = \frac{Y - \bar{Y}}{s_y} =$$

$$r = \frac{\Sigma z_x z_y}{N} =$$

Table C.4 The Pearson *r* Computed from Raw Scores

Subject	X	Y	X^2	Y^2	XY
1					
2					
3					
4					
5					
6					
7					
8					
9					
10					
11					
12					
13					
14					
15					
16					
17					
18					
19					
20					

$\Sigma X =$ $\qquad$ $\Sigma Y =$ $\qquad$ $\Sigma X^2 =$ $\qquad$ $\Sigma Y^2 =$ $\qquad$ $\Sigma XY =$

$(\Sigma X)^2 =$ $\qquad$ $(\Sigma Y)^2 =$

$N = 20$

$$r = \frac{N\Sigma XY - (\Sigma X)(\Sigma Y)}{\sqrt{[N\Sigma X^2 - (\Sigma X)^2][N\Sigma Y^2 - (\Sigma Y)^2]}}$$

Assignment for **EXERCISE C**

1. Compute the Spearman rank-difference correlations between height and weight and between height and the college-aptitude test-score estimates. Prepare the scatter plots for these two sets of data.
2. (Optional) Compute the Pearson product-moment correlation between the height and the weight estimates.
3. Answer the following questions:
   a. Define *correlation* in your own words.

   b. What does a correlation of $-.40$ mean?

   c. What is the difference between the Pearson and Spearman correlation techniques?

82 83 84 85 9 8 7 6 5 4 3 2 1